Biola then

Biola University

Rooted for One Hundred Years

Established 1908

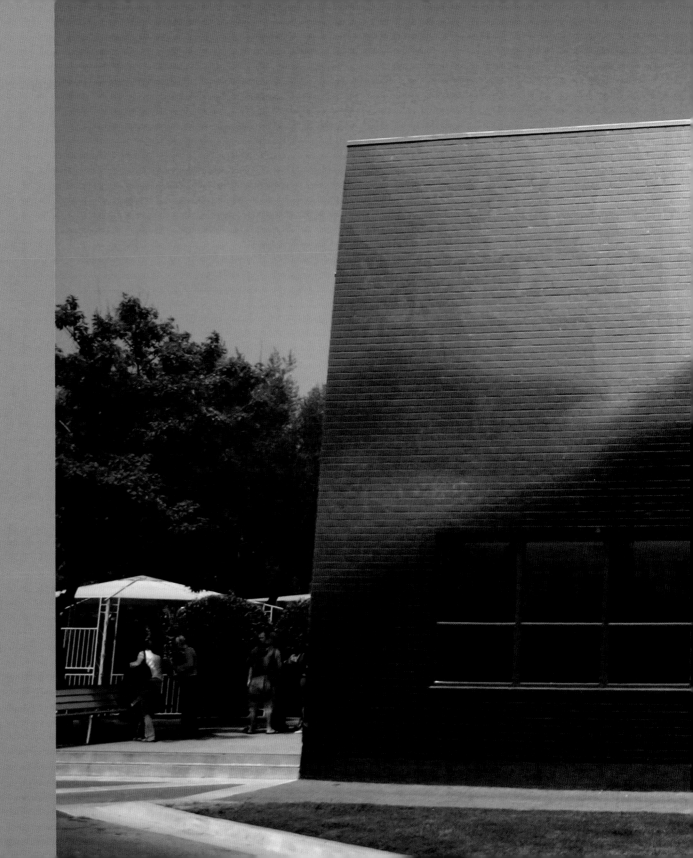

 BIOLA
UNIVERSITY

©2007 Biola University
ISBN-13: 978-0-9799011-6-4

Biola University
13800 Biola Avenue
La Mirada, CA 90639-0001

Printed in China

"The Word" mural

Calvary Chapel

CELEBRATING A CENTURY OF FAITHFULNESS

THIS BOOK REFLECTS upon Biola's heritage and accomplishments in its first 100 years. We trust it provides a renewed inspiration to look forward to a new century remaining faithful to fulfilling Biola's founding mission to impact the world for the Lord Jesus Christ.

Lyman Stewart declared at the Cornerstone ceremony in 1913 (page 18),
> *"these buildings are not to be a monument to any man, but are to forever stand solely for the promulgation of the eternal truths of God's Holy Word."*

Those who make up the Biola community today—alumni, students, faculty, staff, trustees and supporters are called to uphold these poignant words spoken by a Godly visionary.

Reflecting on Biola's past and God's faithfulness instills in us affirmation and the hope that He will continue to direct Biola's future and bring about even greater clarity as we strive for Kingdom impact in all we set out to do to advance the University and the cause of Christ.

We are honored to capture the story of Biola through the following pages. This book is dedicated to the many who have served before us, who are serving now around the world, and those currently in the classrooms learning to impact the world for the Lord Jesus Christ. Because of you, Biola University's mission will continue to unfold into the next 100 years, and prayerfully beyond.

In His Service,

Irene Neller
Senior Director
Integrated Marketing Communications

Brenda Velasco
Centennial Manager
('99)

Wow! What a
year! Thank you
for your great
work!

It has been an
incredible year
and couldn't have
happened without you!

CONTENTS

1970–1982

1982–1997

1997–2008

84

BRANCHING
OUT —
GROWING INTO
A UNIVERSITY

102

A SEASON
OF CHANGE

120

DEEPLY ROOTED
FOR THE NEXT
CENTURY

CHAPTER ONE

Planting the Seed

As the 20th century dawned in Los Angeles, Christians in the growing metropolis faced a mounting challenge. The belief that God could be explained away by science was sweeping the nation. The Western world had become disillusioned with traditional notions of truth and morality and many churches began to supplement old theological creeds and doctrines with modern scientific theories. The result was a cultural movement that became known as "modernism".

GROUNDBREAKING CEREMONY, 1912
The formal groundbreaking ceremony began sharply at 1 p.m. on June 21, 1912. The first spadeful of earth was turned by Lyman Stewart followed by a brief address by T.C. Horton. The ceremony concluded with a hymn: "My hope is built on nothing less than Jesus' blood and righteousness. I dare not trust a sweeter frame, but wholly lean on Jesus' name. On Christ the solid Rock I stand; all other ground is sinking sand," sung by 100 or more students and friends present. T.C. Horton shared a hymnal with R.A. Torrey while Lyman Stewart (arms folded) gazed across the Hope Street site. By 2 p.m. forty workmen were busily attacking the work of excavation for the Institute's new home.

As the modernist movement gained influence in the mainstream culture, Christian beliefs, like the authority of the Bible and the deity of Christ, came under attack. It was at this time that an oil businessman and a pastor teamed up to begin their own counter-cultural movement. Lyman Stewart, co-founder of the Union Oil Company, and the Rev. Thomas Corwin T.C. Horton, a noted pastor and evangelist, opened the Bible Institute of Los Angeles (BIOLA) on February 25, 1908. Their mission was simple: to teach the next generation of believers the fundamentals of the Christian faith, free of cost.

Within two years of its founding, the Institute's student body had outgrown its facility on Main Street and moved to the Temple Auditorium Building at the corner of Fifth and Olive streets. In 1911, the school reached an important milestone as it saluted its first graduating class: six students.

Meanwhile, Stewart and the Institute's directors searched for a suitable permanent home for the school. Stewart had secured a location at the corner of Eighth and Los Angeles streets. But after touring the Moody Bible Institute in Chicago, Stewart felt the land he

> The Bible Institute was now having an impact on the Pacific Coast serving as a visible icon of biblical truth and reaching out to everyday people—from shop and factory laborers to seamen and oil field workers.

The Bible Institute's first student body consisted of 35 students recruited from the Fishermen's Club for men and the Lyceum Club for women established by Horton and his wife, Anna, in 1906. Classes were held on Main Street in downtown Los Angeles. Horton served as the Institute's superintendent, while Anna assisted with teaching and administration. Stewart served as the president of the board of directors.

The Bible Institute was the seed of a broader vision to impact the world for Jesus Christ. In 1909, Stewart and his brother, Milton, funded a multi-volume series of books defending the fundamental beliefs of the Christian faith, aptly titled *The Fundamentals*. Reuben Archer Torrey was selected as the editor of the book project, which would eventually be completed in 1917 and published by the Institute. *The Fundamentals* became the most recognized defense of conservative Christianity at the time. Those who held to the doctrines outlined and defended in the book began to refer to themselves as *fundamentalists*. This term was synonymous with the term "evangelical", until years later when a pejorative use of the term emerged. *The Fundamentals* are still in print with the most recent edition published in 2003 by Baker Book House.

But the Institute became known for publishing well before the release of *The Fundamentals*. For those unable to attend daily classes, Horton decided to publish a regular Institute periodical, *The King's Business*, in 1910, which examined theological and political issues from a conservative evangelical perspective. It fast became one of the largest Christian magazines in the nation with a circulation of up to 200,000. It helped broaden the influence of the young school.

had bought was not going to accommodate the necessary facilities. "We would still have less ground than the Moody Institute," he stated, "while we have an empire to provide for."

News of an exciting prospect came in a letter from Horton to Stewart on September 26, 1911: "We have found a lot, 168 x 180, on the east side of Hope Street which can be bought for $180,000." The deal was too good to pass up and was soon purchased.

In addition to a new site, the growing Institute was also hiring its first dean. Wanting someone with both academic and pastoral credentials, Stewart and Horton approached R.A. Torrey, editor of *The Fundamentals*, who was a respected pastor and evangelist with a pair of theological degrees from Yale College. Torrey had worked closely with famed evangelist, Dwight L. Moody, and served as superintendent of the Moody Bible Institute. Torrey accepted the Institute's offer on the condition that the new school would also establish a church with an auditorium large enough to accommodate at least 3,500 people.

At a simple groundbreaking ceremony on June 12, 1912, the founders dedicated the new site to the Lord. Horton called the proposed building "a rallying center for magnifying the Word of God". Stewart added, "In the name of the Bible Institute, I now take possession of this ground for the Lord's use by the act of turning this spadeful of earth. May our united prayers be that every detail of the construction of this building be accomplished in the fear of the Lord and for His Glory." Torrey, then acting dean, closed the ceremony with prayer.

1908–1924

Hundreds of men worked together to build one of the tallest buildings in the turn of the century in Los Angeles. They hauled concrete up thirteen stories in wheelbarrows, but one tragic accident halted construction momentarily. On May 31, 1914, a construction worker fell from the seventh floor and was killed. The following Thursday a memorial service was held where 400 workers gathered on the floor of the unfinished auditorium to pay their respects. This tragedy turned into a victory as 70 men responded to the "clear, clean-cut gospel message" and turned their lives to Christ.

Construction began immediately on what a *Los Angeles Times* headline called the "Largest Structure Ever Built Exclusively for Religious Education". From a foundation of solid granite, a 13-story building slowly began to emerge, making the Institute the tallest building in Los Angeles.

On May 31, 1913, the founders held a ceremony to set the cornerstone, a piece of granite inscribed with Revelation 1:5—"Dedicated unto Him who loved us and washed us from our sins in His own blood." A copper time capsule containing several dated documents and a copy of Stewart's dedicatory address was placed behind the cornerstone.

Students occupied the edifice in 1914. Soon after, the Institute bought eleven Meneely bells and suspended them atop the north dormitory tower. They were dedicated in July 1915; Mrs. Horton was the first to play them.

Torrey's request for a 3,500-seat church auditorium was fulfilled on September 3, 1915, when the Church of the Open Door officially opened, occupying the space between the Institute's north and south towers. Torrey served as the church's pastor and Horton as assistant pastor.

The Bible Institute was now having an impact on the Pacific Coast serving as a visible icon of biblical truth and reaching out to everyday people—from shop and factory laborers to seamen and oil field workers. During this time, the Biola Press, a thriving department of the Institute, published more than 500,000 printed materials on a monthly basis, including *The King's Business*. The efforts made substantial net profits for the Institute, allowing it to continue expanding its evangelistic work throughout California and abroad.

Overseas, the Institute provided support for Dr. Frank A. Keller's evangelistic work in the Hunan Province of China. Through Keller's endeavors, Stewart became interested in including China in Biola's framework. Officially established in 1916, the Hunan Bible Institute, also called "Biola in China", was instrumental in training Chinese Christians in practical Christian service and doctrine. The Institute sent evangelistic teams known as "Biola Bands", which crisscrossed the country in houseboats, delivering thousands of tracts and New Testaments.

In 1922, the Institute again broke new ground, this time on the airwaves. Its station, Radio KTBI, which broadcasted Biola classes and special meetings, became the first radio station in the country dedicated exclusively to Christian broadcasting.

With finances flourishing, the Institute's leaders held a mortgage-burning ceremony to celebrate paying off the $500,000 debt incurred while building the school.

As the "roaring twenties" dawned, the school thrived. Now debt-free, the Institute's future looked fruitful, holding true to Stewart's vision of being a school in the West preparing men and women for practical Christian service and testimony. ❧

1908–1923

LYMAN STEWART

Lyman Stewart, the founder and president of Union Oil Company and one of the co-founders of Biola University, was born in 1840 in Pennsylvania.

Early in his life, Stewart aspired to buy land rich with oil. After his return from a four-year enlistment with the Pennsylvania Cavalry, Stewart opened an office and negotiated leases and bought part interests in several wells.

Stewart was a man of faith. His strong Christian character impressed the partners of the Claremont Oil Company, so they invited him and his brother, Milton Stewart, to join their company. The six-year partnership earned him $300,000 in savings. He invested his fresh wealth into manufacturing of agricultural machinery and lost it all.

Shortly thereafter, Stewart was approached by Wallace Hardison, a wealthy man interested in investing in oil in the West Coast. After forming a partnership, Stewart in 1882 moved to Los Angeles, where he began to survey land for oil development. In 1888, he and Hardison struck California's first "gusher". Two years later, they consolidated their holdings into one corporation, naming it the Union Oil Company of California.

He focused his interest and resources on a variety of Christian endeavors, including the YMCA and the Gospel Union Mission. Stewart became concerned with the growing movement in American churches toward a social Christianity and away from the lordship of Christ in people's lives. This deep concern caused Stewart and his brother to publish a 12-volume series titled *The Fundamentals*, which urged ministers to return to the essential teachings of Scripture.

In 1895, Stewart offered Thomas Corwin Horton the assistant pastor position at Immanuel Presbyterian Church through the request of Dr. Chichester, pastor of the church. In 1905, they met each other when Horton came to Los Angeles to visit the church and consider accepting the pastorate. They soon became good friends and partners in establishing a Bible training school. Stewart wanted to use his financial resources for the Lord's current work. He did not believe in setting his money aside as endowments.

Stewart can be credited for establishing the Institute financially, yet he understood the need for both corporate responsibility and reliance on the Lord.

Although his goal was to gain financial support from others, he and his brother were required to give of their own money. Records show that Stewart and his brother gave $1,361,000, a huge sum of money at that time.

Even after his death in 1923, Stewart's vision for the Institute held true: a school in the West was preparing men and women for practical Christian testimony and service.

▶ *THE KING'S BUSINESS* MAGAZINE STAFF
T.C. Horton was prompted to publish a regular Bible Institute periodical to convey more information to students and to those who were unable to attend the daily classes. *The King's Business*, Biola's first official magazine, was first published in January of 1910 and was in circulation until 1970. By 1921, over 200,000 foreign and domestic subscriptions were secured.

▲ MR. AND MRS. HORTON
T.C. "Daddy" Horton and his wife Anna "Mother" Horton

▲ WOMEN'S DORM LOBBY
Women of the Bible Institute spent time catching up with friends in the lobby of their dorm.

▲ FISHERMAN'S CLUB MOTTO
On Monday night, April 16, 1906, seven young men met with "Daddy" Horton (as he came to be called) at Immanuel Presbyterian for Bible study and instruction in soul-winning. The class grew to include up to 300 high school and college age men who gathered on Monday evenings. The members of the class selected the name "Fishermen's Club" and adopted Matthew 4:19 as their motto: "And He sayeth unto them, Follow Me and I will make you fishers of men."

CORNERSTONE CEREMONY

On May 31, 1913, Rev. E. P. Ryland, president of the Church Federation, delivered an address at the Institute's cornerstone ceremony, which he congratulated all churches upon the fact that the city is to have an institution founded upon the truth of the Bible. Inscribed upon the polished granite stone were the words from Revelation 1:5, "Dedicated unto Him who loved us and washed us from our sins in His own blood." A copper time capsule was placed under the stone containing a Scofield Bible, copies of *The King's Business*, *What the Bible Teaches* by R.A. Torrey, the Bible Institute Statement of Doctrine, a school catalog and other administrative documents. Lyman Stewart after delivering an address placed the box in the niche prepared for it, with a trowel placed mortar under the huge stone which was then lowered into place. Dr. Torrey, delivered an address on the general work of the institution. He declared that it is founded upon a belief in every book, chapter and verse of the Bible. The cornerstone now lays at the Torrey Plaza at the Church of the Open Door in Glendora, Calif.

1908–1932

T.C. HORTON

The Rev. Thomas Corwin Horton, the second member of Biola University's co-founding team, was born August 3, 1848, in Cincinnati, Ohio. As a young man, Horton accepted Christ as his savior, became active in church and was eventually ordained by the Presbyterian Church. Later, he moved to Indianapolis, where he entered business, became rather successful and met his wife, Anna. At the age of 27, he gave up his business career to enter full-time Christian work with the Young Men's Christian Association.

The geographical scope of Horton's life work extended from the Atlantic to the Pacific Coast. As one of the early pioneers in YMCA work, he served as secretary of various branches of the association in Indianapolis, St. Paul and Dallas. Meanwhile, he received theological training under the scholarly supervision of Dr. Arthur Pierson.

T.C. Horton met Lyman Stewart in the summer of 1905 when Stewart—given the charge to find an assistant pastor—offered him the position of assistant pastor of Immanuel Presbyterian Church under the pastor's direction. Horton accepted the position and moved to Los Angeles in January 1906. For the next 17 years these two men walked arm-in-arm in dedicated service to that which God had called them.

Greatly concerned with the urgent need of bringing men to a saving knowledge of Christ, Horton and other members of a young men's Bible class at Immanuel Presbyterian Church organized the Fishermen's Club in 1906, soon after arriving to Los Angeles. Horton, better known as "Daddy" Horton, became well known for his works on evangelism and personal devotion. His wife, who came to be known as Anna "Mother" Horton, formed the Lyceum Club, a similar group for young women. Initially, the group met in the rug department of the Fifth Street Department Store.

Over the following years, T.C. Horton worked energetically with the Fisherman's Club, did the work of an evangelist, taught Bible classes and worked with Stewart to establish and oversee the Bible Institute. After Horton had success with conducting training classes for Sunday school teachers he discussed the idea of a Bible training school with his friend Stewart.

It has been said of Horton that "he did the leg work" in establishing the school, while Stewart backed him with prayer and finances.

Horton was a man of deep convictions and uncompromising loyalty to the whole Word of God. His vigorous and dominant personality combined the rare qualities of sweetness and strength with deep spirituality and intense practicality. He often stated, "If I had a drop of blood in my veins that was not loyal to Jesus Christ, I would let it out." He passed away on February 27, 1932.

1911–1928

R. A. TORREY

Reuben Archer Torrey, the son of a banker, was born in New Jersey on January 28, 1856. He entered Yale College at age 15 intending to become an attorney. After three years of worldly involvement, he trusted Christ as his Savior and decided to enter the ministry. In 1875, he graduated with honors and that fall entered Yale Divinity School.

In Torrey's senior year, D.L. Moody, the great evangelist, spoke in chapel. Moody taught Torrey how to lead people to Christ. The experience transformed his attitude toward ministry.

After graduation from seminary, Torrey was ordained by the Congregational Church and served as a pastor in Ohio, where he met his wife. Torrey then attended graduate school in Germany, where he came to the firm belief that the Bible was the inspired and inerrant Word of God.

His expansive background molded him into a man who could handle himself and the Bible well, whether on skid row or among theological scholars.

When Moody was searching for a superintendent for his proposed Bible Institute in Chicago, he was advised to secure Torrey, which he did. Torrey designed the curriculum for the new institute, which became the pattern for many all over the world.

In the summer of 1911, Torrey was invited to be the new dean of the Bible Institute of Los Angeles. He had two stipulations. First, he requested a church be organized to function in partnership with the Institute, much like the Moody Memorial Church did with Moody Bible Institute. Second, he asked that the auditorium of the Institute and church be able to accommodate at least 3,500 people for evangelistic services. Torrey accepted Biola's offer the same year.

He gained a most enthusiastic reception on the part of the Institute faculty and student body. *The King's Business* stated, "The coming of Dr. Torrey to our Bible Institute marks a new era in the progress of our work…When we felt the need and commenced to pray for a dean, we asked of the Lord the best man available for such an important position, but we had not thought the Lord would give us the biggest as well as the best."

Under his direction the Institute became widely known as a well-equipped, well-staffed and well-conducted Christian school. Torrey's vision for the Institute, in addition to specialized biblical training, was to unite theory and practice in Christian activity. One of his noteworthy achievements was the Board of Directors' adoption of a clear and concise Statement of Doctrine.

▲ BELL TOWER ATOP LOS ANGELES BUILDING

Eleven Meneely bells, then the largest set of chimes on the Pacific Coast, were suspended atop the north dormitory tower and were first played by "Mother" Horton on July 4, 1915. Later, Dr. Gordon Hooker served Biola and the Church of the Open Door as carilloneur.

▶ GORDON HOOKER

Dr. Gordon Hooker had the task of playing the bells atop of the Institute's 13-story building three times a day and twice on Sunday for thirty-four years commencing in 1926.

◀ LOS ANGELES BUILDING IN 1920

The completed home of the Bible Institute of Los Angeles, circa 1920. Considered a "skyscraper" during that time, the building was labeled as one the architectural achievements of the United States. The "best meal in the city" at the time, was only 25 cents.

1908–1924

◄ CARBARN TEAMS, JANUARY 1923
These men of the Bible Institute made up the Carbarn Team of 1923.

▶ LYCEUM CLUB
In 1907 Mr. D. H. Steele, the owner of the Fifth Street Store in downtown Los Angeles, proposed to Mrs. Thomas C. Horton to teach a Bible class to the young women who worked at his store. After prayerfully considering it, "Mother" Horton formed the Lyceum Club for the young women, and rooms were provided in the store. The name "Lyceum" was inspired by the grove at Athens where Aristotle taught.

▼ TWELVE WOMEN OF THE LYCEUM CLUB
The Bible Women, selected from the Lyceum Club, was organized by Mrs. Anna Horton to win others to Christ by visiting homes and teaching neighborhood Bible classes.

▲ EVANGELISM

In 1917, the Bible Institute of Los Angeles reported 6,491 evangelistic meetings were held; 9,912 classes were taught; 17,056 Bibles, Testaments and Gospels were distributed; 213,650 tracts were circulated, 4,009 Christian books were given away; 48,658 interviews were conducted and 4,756 individuals professed newfound faith in Jesus Christ. The Bible Institute's first graduate, Britton Ross went on to evangelize throughout the United States.

◀ BIOLA IN CHINA

The evangelistic work of Dr. Frank A. Keller in the Hunan Province of China drew Stewart to subsidize his work through the Bible Institute. In 1916, Stewart arranged the administrative transfer, and the Hunan work was incorporated into the Institute's framework as a new evangelistic department. Under Biola's direction, the Hunan Bible Institute, commonly called Biola in China, was established, and Chinese evangelistic teams, known as Biola Bands, were organized.

MINISTERING TO THE HARBOR WORKERS

In 1913, Biola graduate Oscar Zimmerman commenced the Harbor Work, a ministry to sailors and shipyard workers at nearby Terminal Island in San Pedro. Biola Hall, a street mission, soon opened in the port town, and it was not long before the work was also introduced in San Francisco Harbor, where many more international seamen were exposed to the Gospel. A ministry to dock workers was just one of the vibrant evangelistic efforts borne of the Institute. Other ministries during these early years included the door-to-door evangelism of the Bible Women and outreaches to local Jews, Mexicans, oil field workers, and shop and factory laborers. Keeping with Biola's intensely practical approach to training Christian workers, ministry was a mandatory part of the curriculum.

◀ BIOLA PRESS

The Biola Press, a fully-equipped printing plant owned and operated by the Bible Institute became another thriving department of the school. In addition to increased regular press runs of 100,000 or 200,000 copies of *The King's Business*, the plant also accepted commercial orders from other religious institutions. Profits netted from such jobs were applied to the work of the Institute. In 1917 alone, over 7,100,000 pieces of Christian literature rolled off the Bible Institute presses.

▼ CHURCH OF THE OPEN DOOR

R.A. Torrey was so impacted by the church-school collaboration of his former employers, Moody Bible Institute and Moody Church, that he made a stipulation before accepting the deanship of the Institute. He announced that he would come to Los Angeles only if a church were established in conjunction with Biola. Thus, on September 15, 1915, 86 men and women from all over the greater Los Angeles area signed the charter of the Church of the Open Door. The non-denominational congregation used the same facilities as the Institute, and Torrey was pastor until his retirement in 1924. During his tenure, the church grew to over 1,000 members.

▶ FOYER CLASSROOM

By 1916, the curriculum developed allowing students to select and pursue one of four specialized majors. Options included courses in Christian education, missions, music or the "regular course", which focused wholly on the study of the English Bible. Students who were unable to attend day classes could enroll in the Institute's evening school or correspondence course, leading to a certificate upon completion. In 1921, the Institute inaugurated a three-year course designed to give additional training to students who were preparing to become pastors. The student admission regulations were also revised allowing both men and women to enter the school at age 18, abolishing two former limits of 21 years for men and 20 years for women.

▲ FIRST GRADUATING BIOLA CLASS, 1911
The first Institute graduates, left to right top row: Paul Ruske, Elliot Barrett, Andrew Johnson; seated: Helen Day, Thomas Hanney and Helen Smith.

▶ FACULTY, 1917
Dean of the Institute R.A. Torrey and the Biola Faculty of 1917. Seated from left to right: Superintendent T.C. Horton; Torrey: Mrs. Baldwin; John Hunter, Bible teacher and Mrs. Frances Allison, Superintendent of Women. Standing; William Evans, Associate Dean; H.J. Baldwin, Superintendent of Men and music teachers John Trowbridge and Charles Marsh.

CHAPTER TWO

Surviving the Drought

By the early 1920s, Los Angeles was fast becoming a leading cultural center. The town of Hollywood, annexed by the city in 1910, was now producing 800 motion pictures a year, giving the city the name "Tinsel Town". People from all over the country were flocking to the city to work for its movie studios and growing aviation industry. By 1924, the Los Angeles population had grown to more than one million.

BUT JUST AS THE STARS were beginning to shine in Hollywood, Biola's founders were reaching their twilight years. In 1923, Stewart passed away at the age of 83. The following year, Torrey retired as dean and Horton retired as superintendent. Biola was in transition and about to face another challenge.

In 1925, the Scopes Monkey Trial caused a national sensation, testing a Tennessee law that forbade the teaching of evolution in a state-funded school. At this time when sharp lines were being drawn between modernists and fundamentalists, controversy quickly erupted over a statement made by John MacInnis, the school's new dean.

Seeing the advantage of establishing a president, Board members also added a new dean to the administration. Their choice was Dr. Elbert McCreery, a longtime missionary and Bible translator.

The new leadership team faced immediate hardships. Western Machinery Co.—one of the school's investments—declared bankruptcy, plummeting Biola further into debt. The Wall Street Crash of 1929 only made matters worse. Without an endowment, Biola began selling off its assets. The Biola Press went first, then the influential radio station, KTBI. To cut costs, faculty and staff members were given two months of unpaid vacation.

BY 1931, THE GREAT DEPRESSION GRIPPED THE NATION. WITH THE PRINTING PRESS AND BROADCASTING STATION GONE, THE ONLY THING LEFT TO GIVE THE BANKS WAS THE STATELY WHITE BUILDING ITSELF.

MacInnis, a Presbyterian pastor, Biola faculty member and close associate of Torrey's, said that although he agreed with the biblical account of creation, he believed the account was not specific as to the time and manner of creation. This angered some conservatives who felt MacInnis was giving too much ground to supporters of evolution.

Two years later, MacInnis wrote *Peter the Fisherman Philosopher: A Study in Higher Fundamentalism* to the ire of prominent fundamentalists, who denounced it as liberal theology.

The turmoil resulted in a vote by Biola's Board of Directors to determine MacInnis' future at the school. MacInnis received a vote of confidence from the Board, but school donors pressured the Board to remove MacInnis. While leaders at the Institute defended MacInnis' intentions and hesitated to let him resign, he left the school in 1928.

With the taint of controversy hovering over them and rising debt emerging from its operations and decline in donations, leaders at the Institute reorganized the school's administrative structure and enlisted its first president, Dr. William White (1929–1932). A well-known speaker and leader in evangelical circles, White roused the Biola community with his oft-repeated mantra: "The Institute shall not die, but live and declare the works of the Lord."

By 1931, the Great Depression gripped the nation. With the printing press and broadcasting station gone, the only thing left to give the banks was the stately white building itself. That year, the school agreed to lease the north wing of campus—home to the men's dormitories—to the Willard Hotel Company.

When President White departed in 1932, hope came in the form of a warm-hearted Australian immigrant named Louis Talbot, the school's second president (1932–1935). A graduate of Moody Bible Institute and a seasoned pastor, Talbot arrived at a time when Biola's outreach efforts were vibrant, but its future was bleak.

It was under Talbot's leadership that Biola placed a large neon sign on top of the school's north tower, which read "Jesus Saves". The sign became a Los Angeles icon and sent a message of hope to all those facing the challenges of that period. Talbot also took his message of hope to the airways, launching the *Bible Institute Hour*, a weekday Bible study program aired on a borrowed station.

After three years as president of Biola, the amiable preacher stepped down from the presidency to focus on his work as pastor of the Church of the Open Door.

Dr. Paul W. Rood (1935–1938), former president of the World Christian Fundamentals Association, succeeded Talbot in 1935. A visionary, Rood outlined a plan for eliminating Biola's debt within three years while expanding its programs and outreach.

1924–1938

The school did just that. Amid a gloomy financial outlook, Biola thrived as a spiritual beacon in Southern California and around the world. The Institute had already developed a weeklong Missionary Conference beginning in 1929, in which Christian workers from around the globe interacted with students. In 1936, Rood inaugurated the Torrey Memorial Bible Conference, another weeklong event that drew overflow crowds to the school's 4,064-seat auditorium. Both traditions continue today.

Under Rood's leadership, in 1936, Biola also began granting four-year degrees—Bachelor of Theology for men, the Bachelor of Christian Education for women and the Bachelor of Music for both men and women. Over 400 students were enrolled. The baccalaureate program consisted of a year of advanced postgraduate work supplementing the three-year Institute program.

But Biola's financial problems persisted toward the end of the decade. In 1938, when the school was threatened with foreclosure, the Institute's attorney, Claude Watson, proposed a plan to file bankruptcy. Fearing that they might be held personally responsible for the debts, four of the board members resigned. The further test came that same year when the Farmers and Merchants Bank demanded that Biola pay $200,000 of its $700,000 debt within two weeks.

For Talbot, pastor of the Church of the Open Door, bankruptcy was not an option. To rescue the school from its mounting debt, the pastor urged his congregation to buy the auditorium from the Institute. After haggling with banks, a generous agreement was finally reached; the lenders would allow the Institute to keep the facility if they raised a $25,000 down payment within two weeks.

Though the new price was miniscule in light of the original debt, the Depression had ravaged the congregation. Raising

the sum would be a miracle in itself. But Talbot rallied church members around the goal, and *The King's Business* sounded a cry to Institute friends near and far. For weeks, sacrificial donations poured in from around the world. Families dropped cash, heirlooms and even an engagement ring into the offering chest at the church's altar.

When the deadline finally arrived, an announcement appeared in the Church of the Open Door's bulletin:

Victory!
The Goal Reached! $25,365.47 Cash Received
To Make Down Payment!

Though the torrents of controversy and financial trouble threatened to undo the young Institute, the prayers and sacrifices of thousands of faithful individuals enabled the school to weather the storm.

Confident that Talbot could guide the Institute once again, Rood resigned from the presidency in 1938 and Talbot began a second term as the school's president (1938–1952).

As the 1930s drew to a close, the Institute had reached solid ground and was poised for a period of unprecedented growth, led by Talbot whose nurturing hand would continue to guide the school through it all. ✺

▲ JOHN MACINNIS CONTROVERSY
Before heated controversy broke out in 1928 over John MacInnis' book, *Peter the Fisherman Philosopher: A Study in Higher Fundamentalism*, the dean maintained a healthy faculty. In the months after the board accepted the dean's resignation, half of the Bible faculty, several board members and various Biola employees also resigned in protest.

◄ THE GREAT DEPRESSION
Many of the Institute's supporters sustained enormous losses during the Depression, and as a result, donations dropped drastically. The school had been deep in debt before the turn of the decade even though it had experienced a reprieve from debt in the 1920s, and the new directors would be forced to reduce the school's budget to include only the most basic operational costs. Even the Institute building was put up for sale; however, no suitable agreement was reached.

▲ A THRIVING DEPARTMENT

Crates of testaments and tracts destined for India line the sidewalk in front of the Institute. With a national clientele, the press filled orders for a variety of religious institutions.

▲ *THE KING'S BUSINESS* PUBLICATION

Biola Press' primary work was producing *The King's Business*, a monthly publication with a circulation of up to 200,000. Individuals from around the world subscribed to the periodical, which included Sunday school literature, Bible lesson outlines from T.C. Horton and news from each department of the Institute. Publication continued from 1910 until 1970. During the financial turmoil of the Depression, the cash-strapped institute sold the press, but publications like *The King's Business* thrived for decades to come.

◀ A GARDEN ON THE ROOF TOP

The Institute housed a garden on the top of the central auditorium building. A student favorite, the roof garden was a retreat for all.

1924—1938

◄ SOCIAL HALL

Even though Lyman Stewart's purpose for the Institute was to "train young men and women who will evangelize the entire coast through the mining camps and villages and give the Gospel to all people," students still made time to fellowship with one another, building the Institute's inner community.

▲ LECTURE ROOM

One of the more significant educational developments at the school was the inauguration of what was called the "Collegiate Course" in 1936. First mention of this program was made in early 1930, when Dean, Dr. McCreery proposed the program which was approved by President White. However, the board was very skeptical, at first, about venturing into this new area. They wanted to consider every angle to make certain that the founders' original intent would not be violated, so the plans progressed slowly until 1934. After Dr. McCreery presented a revised plan that with certainty would not compromise the founders' intent, the board agreed and filed for a change in Biola's incorporation. The new degrees were granted at the June 1936 commencement: The Bachelor of Theology for men, the Bachelor of Christian Education for women, and the Bachelor of Music for both men and women.

◄ DEFAULT ON A LOAN

In May 1931, officials realized they could not make regular monthly payments to local banks, and for the first time, the Institute defaulted on an obligation. Endeavoring to further reduce the budget, administrators entered a lease agreement with the Willard Hotel Company, relinquishing the north wing of campus.

BIOLA RADIO

The Institute's relationship with broadcasting started shortly after Biola—and radio itself—was born. Biola's chief engineer, M.E. Carrier, proposed the idea of beaming the Gospel over the airwaves just a year after the first public-use AM radio station was established in 1921. Though the idea first met skepticism from R.A. Torrey and T.C. Horton, the school constructed a 10-watt radio transmitter and began broadcasting on March 22, 1922, under the call letters KJS. The school changed the call letters to KTBI (representing The Bible Institute) in 1925. It was the first strictly religious station licensed in the U.S., broadcasting devotional and doctrinal classes as well as a nightly children's program. When the Great Depression struck, the station was sold for $37,500 to KFAC, known then as "The Music Station of Los Angeles". Realizing the importance of the radio, the Institute quickly resumed many programs by buying airtime on KFAC. Although the sale of the station was considered a financial necessity, many were deeply concerned about the loss of this powerful and innovative ministry. Charles Fuller, then chairman of the board of Biola, took action. He arranged with CBS for a half-hour program of gospel music and preaching known as "The Pilgrim's Hour". Carried on several west coast stations, the program was completely financed by Fuller, without cost to the school. But the burden proved too heavy for Fuller and by the end of 1931, he was forced to discontinue the broadcasts.

1929–1932

W.P. WHITE

Dr. William P. White graduated from Monmouth College in Illinois and from Xenia Seminary in Pennsylvania. He held three pastorates, spanning a period of 30 years.

His offer to take the presidency at the Bible Institute of Los Angeles was contingent upon an amicable agreement with Moody Bible Institute where he served as the Pacific Coast representative. The school installed White on June 14, 1929.

As the first president of the Institute, White worked tirelessly to buttress the Institute against the growing debt. He sparked several fundraising efforts with the help of the Board, but those were foiled by the sinking Depression economy. Nevertheless, White's signature proclamation was, "The Institute shall not die but live and declare the works of the Lord." He served the Institute during a time of extreme unrest and difficulty.

He tendered his resignation on September 16, 1932, but remained as president emeritus and editor of *The King's Business*. Relinquishing both titles after six months, White then was appointed Biola's representative in the Pacific Northwest, a position he held for eight years.

SEPTEMBER 1939

The Bible Institute of Los Angeles student body.

SEPTEMBER, 1939.

1935–1938

PAUL ROOD

Paul W. Rood was born of Scandinavian immigrant parents in 1889 and spent his early life in poverty in the Pacific Northwest. At the age of 14, Rood dedicated his life to Christ during an interdenominational evangelistic campaign. Felt called to the ministry, Rood in 1908 entered the North Park College and Seminary in Chicago.

While in Chicago, Rood became involved in urban missions and public evangelism. He later assumed the pastorate of congregations in St. Paul, Seattle, Turlock (Calif.), and Chicago. Passionate about defending biblical orthodoxy in America's pulpits and seminaries, he was elected president in 1929 of the World Christian Fundamentals Association (WCFA), the umbrella organization of the fundamentalist movement, and served in that role during his shortened life.

It wasn't just his dispensational fundamentalism that caught the attention of the struggling Bible Institute of Los Angeles—it was his sense of humor, emphasis on soul-winning, and loving spirit of partnership across theological and denominational lines.

Rood accepted the presidency of Biola during the school's darkest hour—salaries were three months behind and a million-dollar debt hung over the school. His first act as president was to call a day of prayer, during which classes were suspended and students and faculty prayed for God's provision and direction for the school. A revival among the student body was soon to follow. The annual Torrey Memorial Bible Conference was instituted during his tenure and the massive "Jesus Saves" illuminated signs were erected above the Institute towers.

He resigned as president after four years, believing that the task for which he had been called—to help Biola through the most difficult years of the Depression—had been completed. At the time Rood departed in 1939, salaries were up to date and the overall debt had been reduced to $300,000.

Rood continued a very public life of international evangelism until he suffered a massive stroke in 1950, then passed away in 1956. His legacy continues today at Biola through his grandson Paul Rood II, who serves as a professor in the history department.

The Biola Book Room, which originated at the Main Street location, and was a supplier of Christian literature, grew to attract a national clientele and provided the school with textbooks.

▲ CHARLES FULLER, 1921 GRADUATE

With a strong emphasis on missions, the Church of the Open Door witnessed seven of its charter members commit to full-time overseas ministry within a year of its inauguration. Other notable church members include Cameron Townsend, founder of Wycliffe Bible Translators, and Charles Fuller, host of "The Old-Fashioned Revival Hour" radio broadcast and founder of Fuller Theological Seminary.

◄ TORREY MEMORIAL BIBLE CONFERENCE

Shortly after accepting the presidency of Biola, Dr. Paul Rood established a conference dedicated to Bible exposition and named it in Torrey's honor. The Institute cancelled all classes for a week during the event, allowing students to focus exclusively on the sessions. To this day, the conference continues as a three-day event in the fall, drawing nationally renowned speakers to the campus.

1924 — 1938

▲ "THE BIOLA HOUR"

As the Great Depression deepened, all America suffered hard times and the Institute was no exception. Banks were threatening foreclosure on the school's facilities. Most Biola board members felt that the radio ministry should not be reinstated. Dr. Louis Talbot, newly appointed president of the Institute disagreed. Sensing that radio was effective in conveying the Gospel and in reaching a larger constituency, he broadcast programs at his own expense. On November 16, 1932, Dr. Louis Talbot began weekday radio Bible studies known as The Bible Institute Hour, and later "The Biola Hour". In addition to providing sound, verse-by-verse teaching, the program forged an audience support base that provided more than $20,000 hard earned dollars that kept Biola afloat through the Depression.

◀ JESUS SAVES SIGNS

These two seven-foot-high red neon signs were visible for miles and became Los Angeles landmarks. The first was constructed in 1935 with funds from Miss Ramage, a Biola radio listener from Riverside, and a second was added later with gifts from Daniel Rose, who would later lead the Church of the Open Door's Jewish department, and Ray Myers, who would head Biola's board of directors. After an evening service in February 1935 nearly 3,000 gathered to hear three trumpets on the rooftop play, "We have heard the joyful sound, Jesus saves, Jesus saves!" The great crowd began to sing and the sign was turned on for the first time. The "Jesus Saves" signs remained aglow atop the two dormitories until 1985.

◀ FISHERMAN'S CLUB

The Fisherman's Club continued to expand not only in numbers, but also in breadth of ministry. As it became more widely known throughout the area, youth pastors began to solicit the aid of the Fishermen in conducting or speaking at youth meetings. In January 1926, new articles of incorporation were secured from the State of California designating the group as "The International Fishermen's Club". These articles gave power to the corporation to establish and issue charters to additional branches in a variety of areas. As a result, groups of Fishermen were meeting not only in Los Angeles, but in locations throughout the United States, and such foreign places as Palestine and Puerto Rico.

1924—1938

▲ MUSICAL ENSEMBLES

Student musical ensembles, including award-winning men's and women's glee clubs, were as prominent in the 1920s and 1930s as they are today. In addition to performances on campus and off campus tours, Biola vocalists performed to a national audience through KTBI radio.

◀ STUDENT LIFE

Amidst the financial woes of the Institute and the nation's economic status students still found time to enjoy themselves spending time with one another building their friendships.

CHOIRS AND MISSIONARY CONFERENCE
Spring performance of combine choirs and orchestra in 1937. Dr. Herbert G. Tovey, Director, is standing, front center and Dr. Paul Rood is to his right. To stimulate further global awareness, Dr. Philpott, the third pastor of the Church of the Open Door, initiated a large-scale missionary conference during the Easter season of 1930. The conference, though shortened from one week to three days, takes place every spring at Biola and allows students to interact personally with missionaries from around the world.

MORTGAGE BURNING CEREMONY

Dr. Talbot was convinced the Bible Institute should not be victim to bankruptcy or foreclosure. He urged the Church of the Open Door to assist with raising money for the school. After collaboration with Farmers and Merchants Bank as well as Mrs. Lyman Stewart, Talbot reached a compromise. The bank would accept the Institute's 4,000 shares of Union Oil stock in addition to $25,000 cash. After Talbot shared the good news with his congregation and made appeals over the radio to raise the $25,000 he received correspondence from a woman stating, "I have limited strength and small salary and cannot give any money but I am sending my engagement ring which was given to me twenty-nine years ago." On Wednesday, August 3, Farmers and Merchants Bank was presented with payment in full. Bank employees were astounded by the Bible school's ability to raise the money in such a short period. More than 4,000 people filled the Church of the Open Door auditorium on September 11, 1938. A jubilant Louis Talbot burned papers representing more than $700,000 of Bible Institute indebtedness. Through the sacrifices of Biola's friends and members of the Church of the Open Door, the school avoided losing its building to lenders.

1924—1938

CHAPTER THREE

Cultivating the Institute

On April 15, 1938, Superman made his first appearance in the premiere issue of *Action Comics*. The country needed a hero. Americans, already suffering from the Great Depression, had just experienced the Recession of 1937, which had almost wiped out the Bible Institute.

OUTREACH MINISTRIES

Herbert Tovey (not pictured) was appointed Director of Music in 1930, a position he held for 20 years. Musical groups from the Institute and the Church of the Open Door ministered in the streets of Los Angeles. Students were dedicated to full time ministry while enrolled at the school. Outreach thrived with students participating in child evangelism, seaside ministries, women's study groups, and Jewish outreach, all familiar to local residents.

BUT BIOLA HAD ITS OWN HERO in President Louis T. Talbot who helped rescue the school from bankruptcy. Under Talbot, enrollment numbers were climbing once again and the atmosphere at the school was charged with new energy. Although it didn't have much money, the Bible Institute did have a reputation as a leader in practical, hands-on ministry.

The Institute's 450 students were required to participate in evangelism and Christian service in and around Los Angeles. Ministries were diverse and effective. The school's Jewish ministry shared Jesus as Messiah during services on Friday nights and Saturday afternoons. There were numerous outreaches to industrial shop workers and prison inmates. And a

A Japanese-American student, who was forced to move to an internment camp at Santa Anita racetrack in Arcadia, Calif., used the situation to evangelize fellow Japanese-Americans. He wrote to his friends at Biola: "You see I have a tremendous field right before me. I average as much as 10 to 12 miles a day doing pastoral calling, and at present my shoes are just about worn out."

Overseas, bombings and government interference silenced some of the Institute's evangelistic work, but the school continued to make an impact during wartime. In China, the Hunan Bible Institute continued to educate its students, while providing a safe haven for soldiers as they passed through. But by the war's end, China's new Communist

> UNDER TALBOT, ENROLLMENT NUMBERS WERE CLIMBING ONCE AGAIN AND THE ATMOSPHERE AT THE SCHOOL WAS CHARGED WITH NEW ENERGY. ALTHOUGH IT DIDN'T HAVE MUCH MONEY, THE BIBLE INSTITUTE DID HAVE A REPUTATION AS A LEADER IN PRACTICAL, HANDS-ON MINISTRY.

hospital team made weekly visits to the Los Angeles County General Hospital to present flowers, encouragement and the gospel message.

The fruits of these efforts were meticulously documented. In the fall of 1940 alone, the school's Practical Christian Work department tallied 112,956 tracts distributed and 801 professed conversions.

Just when it seemed the Institute was back to normal—having survived controversy and financial crises—the Imperial Japanese Navy launched a surprised attack on Pearl Harbor on December 7, 1941. America was now at war.

The war brought many changes to the Institute. The number of students immediately dropped as many young men volunteered to join the military. And the national Torrey Memorial Bible Conference was cancelled due to gas rationing and travel restrictions.

When Los Angeles became a key port for Navy seamen, the Institute and the Church of the Open Door provided accommodations and meals for 60 to 100 servicemen every Saturday night. The Institute also organized a special Bible class for the soldiers, and young people within the church presented New Testaments to those who made professions of faith.

government would seize control of the Hunan property and Biola permanently withdrew from China in 1952.

After the war, millions of returning soldiers were taking advantage of the G.I. Bill, which provided funding for veterans' education. Suddenly, baccalaureate degrees—which were relatively uncommon in generations past—were in high demand. And Biola was flooded with new students. From 1945–1949, enrollment jumped from 400 to 900 students.

During this period of growth, Samuel Sutherland, a Princeton University graduate who became the school's new dean in 1942, started looking for ways to adapt Biola's academic programming to better meet the needs of a nation in flux. He began an education program in partnership with Los Angeles State College to prepare students to teach in California's growing school system. And, in 1945, he helped Leonie Soubirou start the Institute's School of Missionary Medicine, to provide medical missionaries for organizations eager to get back into the post-war mission field. This course contributed greatly to the general missionary work around the world until the demands for more advanced training necessitated another change, resulting in the current Nursing Program, one of Biola's largest programs today.

But then, unexpectedly, Biola received word that the state college could no longer serve as an accrediting agency for Biola's 125-student education program.

1938–1952

Discouraged, Sutherland sought to change Biola's status, presenting President Talbot with a dilemma: Should the school retain its status as an Institute strictly training lay leaders for biblical ministry? Or should it change to a full-service college, not only to continue the teaching program, but to grow other departments as well?

The decision was difficult. Talbot began an extensive survey of alumni from all over the world, asking for their opinions about Biola's impending transformation. Across the board, the response was positive; most supported an expansion.

In 1952, Talbot made a decision with Sutherland's support that would change Biola forever—the Institute would become a college. ✄

◀ STUDENT GROWTH

Despite a depressive decade, enrollment figures at the Institute continued to grow, and the picture of the student body began to change. The median student age had been about 25, now it had dropped to 20. Student demands were different as were societal values. In explaining curriculum expansion to *The King's Business* readers, Dr. Sutherland commented, "Today's needs differ from those which existed in the early period of Institute life…The curriculum of the Bible Institute 25 years ago never would suffice for the needs of the present time."

▶ WORLD WAR II

During World War II, individuals were instructed to black out the windows of their homes to make them less visible in case of a nighttime air raid. Biola followed suit, blacking out the huge skylight that formed the auditorium ceiling. Many servicemen on their way to war passed through the Church of the Open Door during the 1940s. Many were saved and countless were ministered to in various ways, including listening to Dr. Talbot's evangelistic sermons and fellowship hours arranged especially for servicemen. Dozens of soldiers visited the church each week—so many, in fact, that a special Bible class was arranged for them.

WAR AFFECTS STUDENTS

After the attack on Pearl Harbor, numerous Biola students joined the 16.1 million armed forces personnel who would serve the U.S. during World War II. After enrolling in the service, students realized the value of their training and dependence on the Word in war-torn, uncertain settings. One former student, who was serving as an Army chaplain, wrote about his opportunity to bring men to Christ expressing gratitude for his years at the Bible Institute. "I am so glad that I learned to do this kind of work." (This photo, found in Biola archives, was believed to be taken at a serviceman's funeral.)

LOUIS TALBOT

1932–1935, '38–'52

Louis Thompson Talbot, the sixth of eight children, was born in Sydney, Australia, on October 19, 1889. When he was 13, the young boy and his family went to hear an evangelistic message from R.A. Torrey. Little did Talbot know that the dynamic Torrey would someday become his teacher, and that Talbot would one day fill Torrey's shoes as leader of Biola.

Talbot's older brother had attended Moody Bible Institute in Chicago and urged Louis to enroll. At 21, he immigrated to the United States to study at the famous school. He took his first pastorate during his college years, leading the Emmanuel Congregational Church.

He shepherded congregations in Illinois, Iowa, Minnesota and Ontario and married Audrey Hogue, the pretty organ player from his Paris, Tex., pastorate. On January 10, 1932, he took the pulpit of the Church of the Open Door along with an even bigger challenge—the presidency of Biola.

After three years at the helm, Talbot stepped down from the presidential post and Dr. Paul Rood took over. Three years later, he reassumed the office for another 14-year term.

During two terms as Biola's president, Talbot gained a reputation as an approachable and personable leader with a thorough grasp of Scripture. He shared that wisdom over the airwaves, hosting "The Biola Hour" during the broadcast's heyday in the 1940s.

Though he resigned from the Church of the Open Door pastorate in 1948, he continued on as Biola's president for several more years. His remaining years as president were spent in the general area of public relations and extensive worldwide travel, visiting various missionaries on the field, many of whom were Biola graduates. He resigned in 1952 due to poor health, but remained as chancellor of Biola.

Talbot remained faithful up until his death in 1976. "For this moment I was born," he told his wife before he passed away. "For this I've lived all my life—to see my Savior face to face."

▲ DONATING COINS TO THE INSTITUTE

Donating coins was typical of the sacrificial offering which went into the fund to pay off the building indebtedness. With 3,150 dimes given by a dear Biola friend, here, Mr. Eugene Poole, then director of the Field Department, turns over the coins to Dr. Talbot.

▼ CHURCH OF THE OPEN DOOR'S MISSION

R.A. Torrey named the church based on two passages of Scripture, John 10:9 and Revelation 3:8. The church occupied the center auditorium between the two Bible Institute towers. As an interdenominational church with no motive to compete with other churches, its purpose was to reach the lost of Los Angeles. Dr. Louis Talbot, fourth pastor of the church, witnessed 59 missionaries and 2,000 members added to the church's ministry during his seventeen-year pastorate.

▲ CHURCH OF THE OPEN DOOR

The authority of the Scriptures, the urgency of evangelism, the imperative of prayer and the outreach of missions, all stressed by R.A. Torrey, were the church's major commitments and remain the same. R.A. Torrey led the church from 1915–1924. After nine years of shepherding, the church had grown from 86 to over 1,000 members. Thousands called the church home, and a midweek Bible study led by the congregation's fifth pastor, Dr. J. Vernon McGee, was the largest in the nation during the 1950s. The church continued worshipping in the downtown building even after Biola moved to La Mirada. In 1985, the congregation moved to a new facility in Glendora, where it continues to evangelize.

1938—1952

◀ CHRISTIAN SERVICE

Biola's history has been characterized by students' dedication to Christian service. Students were dedicated to full time ministry even while enrolled at Biola. The majority of graduates were engaged in some type of Christian service.

▼ THEOLOGICAL SEMINARY

Many traditional Protestant seminaries in America changed their statements of doctrine in the 1920s and 1930s. They were taking a "liberal" stand on the basics of the faith. As a result, "fundamentalists" felt that conservative, evangelical seminaries were too few and far between, so the demand for theological schools increased. The Institute's administrators met this need by adding the Bible Theological Seminary of Los Angeles in 1943. It was an intense undergraduate course within the existing curriculum serving as a catalyst for the future addition of Talbot Theological Seminary graduate school in 1952.

▶ CHRISTIAN EDUCATION

During his term as president, Dr. Paul Rood encouraged the Christian Education department to focus more on a different kind of mission field—children. Evangelism teams began directing outreach to the youngest people of Los Angeles. At one point, Rood prayed with Irvin Overholtzer about evangelizing to children and out of that was born Child Evangelism Fellowship in 1937.

▼ SERVING THE MILITARY

During World War II the Institute and the Church provided a safe haven for servicemen. Servicemen passed through the church's doors on their way to war. Many were saved and more were ministered to in different ways. At one point, there were up to one hundred servicemen attending Sunday evening service.

▲ LIBERAL ARTS

The curriculum was not meeting the needs of the day. Dean Sutherland stated, "Today's needs differ from those which existed in the early period of Institute life. Graduates meet other young people of whom a large percentage have been educated in the art, science, philosophy, sociology and psychology of this present age." The administrators faced the challenge of heading in a new direction with the same purpose—to train students in liberal arts in addition to the bible.

▲ VEHICLE DONATION

Bob Pierce donated this vehicle to the Bible Institute for the Youth Center work.

1938 — 1952

ASIAN OUTREACH

The Hunan Institute graduated hundreds of Christian workers before the property was confiscated by the communist regime. Biola then refocused its Asian outreach toward missions in Hong Kong, which continued until the school handed the reins of the ministry to Emmanuel Church in 1961.

▶ HUNAN CLOSES

After 43 years of evangelizing to the Chinese, the Hunan Bible Institute was forcefully closed in 1952.

HUNAN BIBLE INSTITUTE

Every year, Biola Bands convened for a Bible conference at the Nan Yoh mountain, where they received training and also witnessed to locals. These gatherings prompted Keller to set up a central location to train Christian workers in doctrine and evangelism. Out of that dream, the Hunan Bible Institute was born in 1916. During the 1920s, the institute constructed numerous permanent buildings in the city of Changsha, supported largely by Biola.

◀ STUDENT OUTREACH
Students were eager to remember and aid alumni, especially those serving overseas. In one act of generosity in 1951, the Student Missionary Union worked diligently to raise funds and purchase a Piper aircraft for missionaries on the field. Other students were occupied with "home missions" and dealt with such domestic problems as the migrant influx in the late 1940s and early 1950s.

▶ BIBLE INSTITUTE LIBRARY

The library during this time contained more than 23,000 readily accessible volumes, including bound volumes of periodicals and a Braille stock of 287 titles, plus more than 1,000 pamphlets and 72 current periodicals. Inter-library loans were also available to students through the Los Angeles Public Library conveniently located next to the Institute.

▲ STUDENT GROWTH

Programs instituted during the 1940s, such as the School of Missionary Medicine and the Education program, drew many new students. Between 1945 and 1949, the student body jumped from 400 to over 900, and existing Biola facilities became more and more inadequate.

▶ LANGUAGE CLASSES

Alumni in foreign missions complained of problems in learning new languages, which prompted Biola to upgrade language and linguistics classes during the late 1940s. Emphasizing phonetics, the new curriculum equipped students to transcribe previously unwritten dialects.

◀ SAM SUTHERLAND

Called "Mr. Biola" by students who knew him, Sam Sutherland was a forward-thinker during his time as dean in the 1940s, and his suggestions often raised eyebrows among faculty and board members. But his vision to expand both the campus and curriculum eventually came to fruition in the decade to follow when he became president in 1952.

▼ MISSIONARY MEDICINE

In underdeveloped countries where students served, the need for practical knowledge grew more and more evident. To meet this need, Biola incorporated the School of Missionary Medicine in 1945. Under the leadership of Miss Leonie Soubirou, students were trained to treat a broad range of diseases they might encounter on the mission field. This program later became the nursing department. (photo circa October 1950)

1938–1952

◀ MUSICAL BIOLANS

Musical groups ministered to various churches in the Los Angeles area.

▼ BIOLA RADIO CHOIR 1952–1953
WITH HERBERT G. TOVEY

The Church of the Open Door and Biola shared a vast music ministry. Since the church installed the pipe organ in 1919, a large choir and orchestra had consistently enhanced worship over the years in the acoustically perfect auditorium. Dr. Gordon Hooker, church pianist from 1926–1966, as well as music directors J.B. Trowbridge, Dr. Herbert Tovey, Mr. Ted Nicols, were some that contributed to the church's musical testimony and the Institute's growing musical program. Some choirs and musical groups were featured on the Biola Radio.

▶ BIOLA RADIO

By 1946, "The Biola Hour" had a national reputation and was broadcast over most of the 183 stations across the United States. After Talbot, several notable Bible teachers hosted the program, including President Sutherland and Dr. Charles Feinberg. After "The Biola Hour" ended, Biola students continued studying the craft of radio through the on campus station KBBK, established in 1977.

▶ **CHOIR**

The School of Music provided vocal opportunities for experience in two types of ensemble: vocal, including the Coronation Choir, Freshman Choir, and the Radio Choir; and instrumental, including band and orchestra. Annually the music department held the Spring Festival of Sacred Music combining various ensembles and personnel of the department.

▼ **BIOLA ON THE RADIO**

A student, David Crane announces Paul Gupta. Gupta, a native of India who attended Biola, returned to his homeland to form the Hindustan Bible Institute. David Crane served as the radio engineer for "The Biola Hour" from 1950–1954.

1938–1952

BECOMING A COLLEGE

Increasingly, mission boards expressed the need for students well versed in liberal arts, as well as in biblical studies, reporting that many countries were much more likely to accept students with college degrees. After World War II, the educational pattern in America had changed drastically as well, making a standard baccalaureate degree program necessary for entrance into nearly any professional field. In 1952, after much deliberation, the Bible Institute became Biola College.

1938 — 1952

CHAPTER FOUR

Transplanting into Rich Soil

In the same year England crowned its new queen, Elizabeth II, the Institute changed its name to Biola Bible College, launched Talbot Theological Seminary with Dr. Charles L. Feinberg, as the founding dean, and inaugurated Samuel Sutherland (1952–1970) as its fifth president. This marked the beginning of a new vision to impact the world for Jesus Christ through higher education.

SURVEYING THE LAND

When deciding on a new home for Biola College, leaders chose a quiet parcel of land in an unincorporated area known as La Mirada. The rolling hills were dotted with olive trees and irrigation lakes, and the only sign of civilization at the time was a tiny railroad station where travelers caught Santa Fe passenger trains. Both Sam Sutherland and Russ Allder surveyed more than two dozen sites, including land in Rose Hills, Burbank, Pasadena, Palos Verdes, the upper San Fernando Valley and several spots in Orange County before they decided on La Mirada.

BUT TO BECOME THE BOLD AND VIBRANT COLLEGE its leaders envisioned, Biola needed more room to expand. By 1952, Los Angeles had become the second largest city in the nation with nearly two million people. In addition, a large number of automobiles in the city, together with the bright sunlight and frequently stagnant air, led to a new kind of pollution called photochemical smog. Both the city congestion and the pollution were among the deciding factors of Biola's move towards a calmer, cleaner suburban city.

With enrollment swelling, the decision was made in 1954 to follow the newly created Santa Ana Freeway south to a 75-acre plot of sprawling olive groves in the Los Angeles suburb of

of Biola's business manager, Russ Allder, who assisted in finding the La Mirada location. The planned city was billed as the as the "up-and-comingest" of L.A.'s suburbs and offered Biola students a tranquil learning environment.

With only two dormitories to accommodate a growing student body, some students had to live in the old downtown building, taking buses to the new suburban campus. In spite of this inconvenience, Biola continued to grow and develop into a full-fledged college.

But one major hurdle challenged Biola's transition from Bible institute to four-year college—the school still needed accreditation. After consulting with Biola's dean, Dr.

WHILE COLLEGE CAMPUSES ACROSS THE NATION ROILED UNDER THE WAR PROTESTS AND CIVIL UNREST OF THE 1960S, BIOLA REMAINED RELATIVELY CALM, HOLDING TO ITS VISION OF EQUIPPING LAY LEADERS AND PREPARING STUDENTS FOR MISSIONS AND MINISTRY.

La Mirada. That same year, Walt Disney broke ground on a citrus farm in Anaheim, Calif., for the construction of Disneyland and business began to expand in Orange County.

Three thousand people attended a groundbreaking ceremony for the new campus on May 26, 1957. Though grass and groves stretched out as far as the eye could see, the crowd buzzed with the same anticipation that accompanied the groundbreaking of 1912. The first shovelfuls of dirt were emotional ones—Biola had just reached a new promised land.

Memories of leaner years—and the near-loss of Biola's downtown building during the Depression—prompted leaders to take a shrewd step in building the new campus. The college committed itself to staying debt-free throughout the process. Although this kept progress sluggish at times, it wasn't long before new buildings arose from the fields. A humble president's house—which later housed the Biola Counseling Center, then the Department of Education and eventually gave way to the Crowell School of Business building in 2006—was first. Then came the multipurpose Ethel Lee Memorial Building, subsequently named Sutherland Hall. The campus was ready to be occupied when a library, science building, dining hall and two dormitories were completed.

In 1959, just one year after the Brooklyn Dodgers arrived in Los Angeles—winning the first world championship on the West Coast—Biola transitioned to its new home in La Mirada. Sutherland and chairman of the Board, Ray Myers led the transition with the help

James Christian, Dr. Sutherland and Dr. Earl Pullius (a University of Southern California professor) made key administrative and curricular changes, including expanding the library holdings, purchasing laboratory equipment, increasing faculty pay, adding more liberal arts courses and developing Biola's athletic programs.

The changes worked and the school officially received accreditation by the Western Association of Schools and Colleges (WASC) on February 28, 1961. And Biola changed its name once again to simply Biola College.

Now an accredited college, Biola entered a season of rapid growth. Between 1961 and 1971, student applications more than doubled from 500 to 1,120. The 50,000-volume library became a 90,000-volume library. And the annual budget jumped from $2 million to $5 million.

Along with the campus community came an abundance of collegiate social events. New traditions emerged, like the Biola Egg, a 200-pound, egg-shaped chunk of cement that residence hall floors have attempted to hunt down or hide from each other. Other memorable activities, such as the Sutherland Sizzle—a picnic breakfast at a nearby park—and "Twirp" parties, which later became "BAB" dates ("Betty Asks Bob"), became social staples still enjoyed by Biola students today.

1952–1970

One of the most popular changes was Biola's decision to join the National Association of Intercollegiate Athletics (NAIA). Before 1962, Biola's athletic department had a limited intercollegiate athletic program. Under the skilled leadership of men such as Ed Norman, who coached soccer and basketball, and J. Richard Chase, the overall athletic program began to thrive, receiving frequent recognition. Athletic Director Robert McCullum worked to develop a highly organized athletic program. By 1962, women's basketball, softball and tennis teams were official sports under the direction of Mrs. Betty Norman.

Optimistic about the future of the school, the Biola community bonded together. When the campus needed landscaping, professors and students teamed up to buy and plant flowers. When the school needed a new gymnasium, athletes teamed up to raise funds for the building. Several faculty members participated actively in city politics of the newly founded city of La Mirada. Dr. David Peters, a new history professor, served on the city council and became La Mirada's mayor five times throughout his tenure and continues to teach at Biola today.

While college campuses across the nation roiled under the war protests and civil unrest of the 1960s, Biola remained relatively calm, holding to its vision of equipping lay leaders and preparing students for missions and ministry. And it was largely due to the faithful, yet ambitious leadership of the man dubbed "Mr. Biola"—Sam Sutherland. ✣

▲ PURCHASING LAND

Before Biola's board members bought the La Mirada land, there were plans to purchase a small parking lot directly across the street from the south dormitory in Los Angeles. Dr. Sutherland's plans consisted of erecting a 13-story building on the parking lot site. Ray Myers, Chairman of the Board, made a deposit of $5,000 to hold the property. As Myers, Sutherland and Talbot met over lunch they discussed the vision for the new structure. After calculating that the structure would cost about one and a half million dollars, Myers stated, "I could build a campus with all of the facilities and then some." Sutherland excited, took Myers up on the offer and charged the men to do it. Their search for land began.

▲ PURCHASED LAND

Initially, 160 acres were purchased in the heart of the then dormant La Mirada. Biola kept 75 acres—50 for the campus and 25 for a housing development, and sold the remainder to help cover the cost of the building project. This project would cost Biola $1.5 million and hours of work and energy.

◀ BOARD MEMBERS SURVEYING THE LAND

Biola board and faculty members were eager to find a home suitable for the growing school. In 1954, board members discovered a plot of 160 acres in the heart of a newly emerging Los Angeles suburb, La Mirada. Publishing magnate Andrew McNally originally owned it. Talbot led the board members as they surveyed the land.

1952–1970

SAM SUTHERLAND

The son of a Presbyterian minister, Dr. Samuel H. Sutherland was born September 4, 1900, in Fulton, Calif. When Samuel was nine years old, the family moved to Sausalito, Calif., where he made his first public confession of faith in Jesus Christ.

After graduating from high school in June 1918, Sutherland enlisted in the United States Army during the climax of World War I, but was released shortly thereafter when the war came to an end. He then entered Occidental College in 1918.

While studying in Los Angeles, Sutherland frequently attended the Church of the Open Door, making him familiar with Torrey's preaching and with Biola. After serving a year at the Pasadena YMCA, he left for Princeton Theological Seminary in 1924. In 1925, Sutherland's senior year, he met Eleanor Stirrett from Toronto, Canada, and married in 1927.

Following his Princeton graduation in 1927, Sutherland returned to Southern California and became pastor of the Grace Presbyterian Church in Highland Park, which T. C. Horton had founded.

Sutherland became director of the Extension Department at Biola in 1936 with a salary of $150 a month. After moving up to the position of director of Christian Service and later to academic dean, Sutherland became Biola's president in 1952.

Under Sutherland's leadership, Biola moved its campus to its current La Mirada location in the summer of 1959. Sutherland and Russell Allder, Biola's business manager, were instrumental in purchasing and developing the new 75-acre campus. With his leadership, the college obtained accreditation by the Western Association of Schools and Colleges.

After 18 years in office, Sutherland's presidency ended in 1970. Through it all, he was seen as a leader who was compelled by conviction, driven by traditional theological views, grounded in God's Word, and gifted with a keen sense of vision—all of which resulted in phenomenal growth for Biola.

◄ WISE INVESTMENTS

Dr. Sutherland's presumptuous idea to purchase the lot across the street of the downtown building paid off large dividends, a net profit of $423,000. The school sold the lot to the Superior Oil Company. Dr. Sutherland and the board members nailed the first stake.

◄ OLIVE TREES

Dr. Sutherland points out the vast underdeveloped land to students. When Biola first purchased the land it was filled with olive trees. Obviously building on the land would mean eliminating most of the trees. However, board members and faculty found it important to maintain the city's rich history, so they kept some trees on campus. Today an olive tree sanctuary remains dedicated to the history of the land.

▲ GROUNDBREAKING

At the groundbreaking ceremony on May 26, 1957, Rev. Bob Shuler gave the keynote address. Pastor of Trinity Methodist Church in Los Angeles, Shuler was a close friend of both Dr. Talbot and Dr. Sutherland. The ceremony bridged two different eras in the school's history—among the 3,000 people present at the ceremony were Mrs. Lyman Stewart, wife of the late co-founder; Edith Torrey, daughter of R.A. Torrey, and T.C. Horton's two daughters.

GRADUATION

By the time Dr. Sutherland announced his retirement in 1970, Biola College was growing in numbers and buzzing with excitement on its new campus. In the late 1960s, Biola was graduating nearly 1,400 traditional students.

CHAPTER FIVE

Branching Out—
Growing into a University

The conclusion of Sam Sutherland's 18-year presidency in 1970 marked the beginning

of what novelist Tom Wolfe famously described as the "Me Decade".

BIOLA College

COMMENCEMENT EXERCISES

SUNDAY, JUNE 5, 3:30PM

FULL ACCREDITATION

The school's next step was to gain full accreditation as an academic institution. The administration sought to initiate changes and additions in the curriculum recommended by the Western Association of Colleges in its preliminary review of the institution. (photo circa 1966)

ESTABLISHED INSTITUTIONS SUCH AS THE FAMILY, the church and the government were being questioned as Americans became preoccupied with self-fulfillment. Divorce, drug use and abortion were all on the rise and church attendance was at an all-time low.

Students protesting the Vietnam War clashed with police on campuses across the country, as the economy was experiencing its worst performance since the 1930s. It was during this turbulent time that Dr. J. Richard Chase (1970–1982) took the mantel as Biola's sixth president.

Times were changing and Chase knew Biola would need to adapt to meet the social and economic challenges facing the school. For the first time in history, there were more women

Meanwhile, a steady progression of new building projects began filling out the empty corners of the sprawling campus. To accommodate the growing number of female students, Sigma Chi, a 285-bed residence hall, was built at the north end of campus. South Hall, originally built in 1970 to house men, was converted into a women's dormitory and renamed Hart Hall in honor of Margaret Hart, who served Biola faithfully for many years as dean of women.

In 1973, the construction of Feinberg Hall provided new classrooms for undergraduate and seminary students, along with faculty offices and a cross-shaped auditorium called Calvary Chapel. A few years later, the nursing program moved into the newly remodeled Soubirou Hall, named in honor of Leonie Soubirou, the founder of the original School of Missionary Medicine.

> SENSING THE OPPORTUNITY FOR BIOLA TO GROW ITS ACADEMIC PROGRAMS, CHASE COMMITTED FROM THE START THAT THE COLLEGE SHOULD NOT BE GUIDED BY PREVAILING FASHIONS IN THE WORLD OF HIGHER EDUCATION, NOR BE PARALYZED BY TRADITION. INSTEAD, BIOLA WOULD SEIZE NEW OPPORTUNITIES WHILE REMAINING TRUE TO ITS ORIGINAL, DISTINCT PURPOSE OF BIBLICALLY CENTERED EDUCATION.

than men attending college. And with a dwindling economy, competition for employment in a diminishing job market became fierce. Now more than ever, students needed an education that provided practical job training.

Sensing the opportunity for Biola to grow its academic programs, Chase committed from the start that the college should not be guided by prevailing fashions in the world of higher education, nor be paralyzed by tradition. Instead, Biola would seize new opportunities while remaining true to its original, distinct purpose of biblically centered education.

But maintaining the proper balance between academics and foundational biblical training was a challenge, especially as colleges became more focused on practical job training.

Biola's requirement that all students complete 30 semester-units of Bible training—essentially two full semesters of theology classes—meant many students had to commit to spending an additional semester or year in school just to finish their undergraduate studies. To alleviate this burden without sacrificing the school's commitment to the Bible training, administrators introduced "interterm", an accelerated session between the fall and spring semesters that allowed students to earn up to four units of credit.

Biola's growing student body, which had exceeded 2,500 students by the late '70s, now needed additional space for faculty and staff. In 1978, construction began on Metzger Hall, a three-story structure, which became Biola's administrative hub. The College also began leasing McNally Junior High School for additional classroom space.

As the campus grew, so did the breadth of Biola's academic programs. In 1977, the College acquired Rosemead School of Psychology and began publishing its *Journal of Psychology & Theology*. With the integration of psychology and theology as its hallmark, the graduate school aimed to alleviate the shortage of well-trained Christian psychologists and became the first Christian university to offer an integrated degree in the U.S.

But an even greater expansion was in store. Wanting to maintain the institution's spiritual distinctives, while growing its academic programs, the Board of Trustees and the school's administration began to wrestle with the idea of becoming a Christian university. The option, advocated by Chase, quickly became apparent as God's direction for the school.

A university framework would offer tremendous opportunities for equipping each student with a specialized proficiency and a broad knowledge base. The Trustees and the

1970–1982

administration agreed that coupling academic strength and the abiding commitment to the Word of God would bear rich fruit for the school and impact lives around the world. The board unanimously approved the change in May of 1981 and Biola College became Biola University on July 1, 1981. Instrumental in this change was Dr. Robert B. Fischer, Provost and Senior Vice President, bringing his vast experience in higher education to help Biola University during this transition.

The change wasn't merely a switching of names; the shift brought a dramatic restructuring to the school. The existing 23 undergraduate majors moved into the new School of Arts, Sciences and Professions. Talbot Theological Seminary joined Rosemead School of Psychology as a graduate school of Biola University.

Students excelled in athletics and academics during Biola's first years as a university. The Biola Eagles soared to success in almost every varsity sport. During the 1982 season, the men's varsity basketball team, coached by Howard Lyon

and David Holmquist, gained national attention when it became the only team in the nation to be undefeated in league play, winning 39 consecutive games.

In academics, the English Department initiated the practice of conducting regular literary symposiums. Further academic strides included the acquisition of an electron microscope by the sciences division, the introduction of a new master's degree in music and the addition of a public relations emphasis within the communications major.

The tremendous changes that characterized the school's first quarter-century in La Mirada set an important precedent for the years ahead. As administrators witnessed a rapidly changing society, they worked hard to implement programs that would more fully address the diverse and pressing needs of a contemporary culture. At the same time, leaders upheld and reinforced the school's commitment to the values that had long set Biola apart—the study and application of the Bible and the emphasis on missions, locally and abroad.

By 1982, the Biola community had reason to celebrate. The school had made the transition from a Bible college to a university—not according to fashion or tradition—but according to the leading of God's Spirit, in step with the vision of its founders. After 12 years as Biola's president,

Chase decided to accept an offer to become president of Wheaton College in Illinois. His successor, Dr. Clyde Cook (1982–2007), would guide the University through some of its toughest challenges and greatest achievements. ❧

▲ AERIAL PHOTO OF CAMPUS IN 1977

By 1977, Biola had grown and expanded in the young city of La Mirada. Built in 1963, the music building, Crowell Hall, named after Mrs. Lyman Stewart's sister, Alice Gray Crowell was fully operational. The music department arranged for artists such as renowned photographer Ansel Adams and fine musicians such as Richard Unfried and Virgil Fox to lecture and perform on campus.

◀ ARIZONA BIBLE COLLEGE

Biola, always looking to extend its educational portfolio, sought to establish itself in yet another location. Arizona Bible College, an independent Bible school in Phoenix, sought financial assistance from Biola, resulting in suggesting that Biola take over operations of the school. Biola did not want to let the opportunity pass, so "Biola in Arizona" was born. The venture brought about many difficulties. With virtually no support, Biola continued with this undertaking for several years, but felt they could not subsidize the school beyond the value of the property. The school closed in May 1971.

J. RICHARD CHASE

1970–1982

Born October 7, 1930, Dr. J. Richard Chase grew up on a large farm—the Chase Brothers' Dairy—a few miles outside of Oxnard, Calif. The product of a strong Christian home, Chase developed a desire to devote his life to serving God while attending Culter Academy, a Christian high school in Los Angeles. It was also in high school that Chase met his wife, Mary Sutherland, daughter of Dr. Samuel Sutherland.

Chase enrolled at Biola in 1948 and graduated with a Bachelor of Theology degree in 1951. After further studies at Los Angeles City College and Pepperdine College, he received a B.A. in Speech Education in 1953 and an M.A. in Speech in 1954. While attending Pepperdine, he taught in Biola's Speech Department. He received a Doctor of Philosophy degree in Speech in 1961 from Cornell University.

During his time teaching in the Speech Department, Chase developed the forensic program at Biola, forming debate teams that competed locally and regionally. After resigning from his teaching position, he was appointed academic vice president in 1955. When the time came for Sutherland to step down from the presidency, Chase was a perfect fit.

He became the University's sixth and youngest president on July 1, 1970.

At his inauguration, Chase expressed his philosophy of a well-balanced Christian school. "There are two tyrants to sound education," he said. "They are tradition on the one hand and fashion on the other."

During his 12-year tenure, Chase initiated several new programs, oversaw the acquisition of Rosemead School of Psychology and transitioned Biola from a college to a university.

Chase served as a good academic navigator, keeping the school on the right course. In the midst of great changes within the school and the nation at large, he cultivated and maintained Biola's commitments to academic excellence and sound Christian teaching. He resigned in 1982 to become president of Wheaton College.

▲ SCHOOL OF MISSIONARY MEDICINE;
LEONIE SOUBIROU

In 1980, Soubirou Hall was named in memory and dedication to Miss Leonie Soubirou's vision. Soubirou directed the School of Missionary Medicine and pioneered the program at the downtown campus. She was both loved and respected by those who attended her classes. The nursing program is one of Biola's largest programs today.

▸ HORTON HALL

In the late '70s the men permanently took residence in Chi Delta, and renamed it Horton Hall.

▲ SIGMA CHI

Since the female enrollment was growing at Biola and across college campuses, Biola needed to construct another female dormitory to meet the demand. Sigma Chi was constructed at the north end of campus. Nicknamed the "Biola Hilton", it had amenities students weren't used to such as suite living with an adjoining bathroom.

◄ METZGER HALL CONSTRUCTION

In 1978, Metzger Hall was constructed meeting the need of a facility that would accommodate additional faculty and staff for the growing student body. About one-half of the project was funded through the estate of Mrs. Adele Metzger.

▲ DR. CHARLES FEINBERG

Dr. Charles Feinberg, initially came to Biola as a Torrey Conference speaker. He joined the faculty in the fall of 1948, as a professor of Old Testament. During this time discussions were swirling about starting a full graduate program. He proposed a standard program offering a three-year Bachelor of Divinity Degree and a four-year Master of Theology degree. In 1952, the Talbot Theological Seminary began with Dr. Feinberg as the first dean, a position he held until his retirement in 1975.

◄ FEINBERG HALL

Work began on Feinberg Hall in 1973. Directly adjacent to the seminary building, Feinberg Hall, named after Talbot's dean Charles Lee Feinberg, provided classroom facilities for both undergraduate and seminary students as well as faculty offices, while the above enclosed sanctuary, called Calvary Chapel, provided an ideal place for daily seminary chapels, meetings and special events.

1970—1982

◀ BIOLA ABROAD

BIOLA ABROAD

Biola Abroad, a program in which students were able to tour various European countries for academic credit, was made available in 1973, under Dr. Reinhard Buss. Biola continues to provide students with over 20 study-abroad programs, from the streets of Los Angeles to the deserts of Cairo, Egypt. They can study in Baja, Alaska, or London. Biola offers a study abroad program for almost all majors.

▼ DONKEY BASKETBALL

One of the special basketball highlights of the year was the Donkey Basketball Game between the Falcons (a student association who promoted school spirit) and the faculty. The tradition continued until the early '80s.

ENROLLMENT INCREASES

From 1971–1979, enrollment nearly doubled from 1,628 to 3,202 students. This growth exceeded the total student body count beyond the maximum predicted figure of 2,500.

SCHOOL'S COMMITMENT

Leaders upheld and reinforced the school's commitment to several distinctives, including the study and application of the Bible as the infallible Word of God and the importance of the Christian mission, locally and abroad.

JOB MARKET

The diminishing job market of the 1970s brought about challenges. With the influx of women in the workforce, competition for jobs increased. More than ever, students needed an education that provided practical job training.

ASSOCIATED STUDENT SERVICES

Biola's Associated Student Council felt the effects of the increased enrollment and reorganized to develop programs to better serve the students. *The Chimes*, student newspaper, and *The Biolan*, the yearbook, were placed under the supervision of the student publications board. The Student Relations Board was created to serve as a liaison between students and administration and the community. Included in student relations were the athletic board, social board, chapel board and the Student Missionary Union (SMU).

◂ ROSEMEAD SCHOOL OF PSYCHOLOGY

In 1977, Biola incorporated the Rosemead School of Psychology into a graduate school. Dr. Clyde Narramore, founder of Rosemead School of Psychology in Rosemead, Calif., proposed that they have a part in the accredited, evangelical institution. Rosemead was the first school to integrate psychology and theology, which is its hallmark even today.

▸ BECOMING A UNIVERSITY

While the board of trustees of Biola agreed that all possible measures should be taken to advance and enrich Biola's academic programs, they also opposed any plan for expansion which would depreciate, minimize or eliminate the historical Christian distinctives of the institution. After much prayer, analysis and evaluation, the concept of a Christian university, championed by the president, became apparent as God's direction for Biola. The transition from college to university was effective July 1, 1981.

▶ ROSE LIBRARY

Built in 1960, the Daniel Rose Memorial Library was possible through the gracious gift from Daniel Rose in memory of Selina and Clara Rose. Daniel Rose and his family fellowshipped at the Church of the Open Door and the Bible Institute. He took over Biola's Jewish department in 1936. He was very involved at Biola. He installed the "Jesus Saves" signs. Construction in 1969 doubled the space to 30,000 increasing study spaces to 340, making room for a student body of 1,500.

▲ LANSING POOL

Lansing pool was built in 1974 in honor of a gift from Louise Lansing (pictured above in pink). It is open year round every afternoon for students and in the morning for lap swimming. Currently classes are offered to become certified as a lifeguard and swim instructor. The pool became an asset for the school when Biola started its competitive swim program in the mid-'90s.

▶ LARGE STUDENT BODY

After Biola transitioned to university it experienced changes throughout campus. The undergraduate colleges came to be known as the School of Arts, Sciences and Professions and Talbot Seminary and Rosemead School of Psychology reorganized as graduate schools. In the fall of 1981, Biola welcomed a student body of 3,100.

1970–1982

▶ RADIO, FILM AND TELEVISION PROGRAM

In 1978, the radio, television, and film (RTF) program began. KBBK goes on air. The now called Cinema and Media Arts program, shot its first film in 1979.

▼ BIOLOGICAL SCIENCE

Two new areas of student involvement were added to the Biological Science department in 1976. 1) The founding of the Biola Science Fellowship for all students interested in the sciences. 2) A Whale Watch training program was started in conjunction with the Cabrillo Marine Museum and the American Cetacean Society. Students were trained to give lectures to schoolchildren both at the various schools and on board the whale watching vessels.

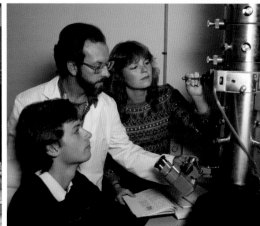

▲ ADDITIONAL UNITS

Biola did not waiver on maintaining the 30 semester units of Bible training in spite of the country's new restructured idea of a university. Biola was placed in the same category as other university's, even ones that did not stress biblical training. The school introduced interterm classes—accelerated classes during winter break.

▲ ELECTRON MICROSCOPE

The Science department acquired an electron microscope.

◀ CHORALE

The Biola Chorale, previously called the Coronation Choir, combines skilled voice with a heart of worshipping God through the art of choral singing. The ensemble is made up of forty-five to sixty students. From 1983–1988, the music department offered a Master's Degree in Music.

◀ FIRST ORCHESTRA PROGRAM

In 1982 Marlin Owen joined the music faculty and began the first orchestral program. The Biola Chamber Orchestra was born, later to be renamed The Biola Symphony Orchestra.

◀ SYMPHONIC WINDS

The National Association of Schools of Music granted the Music department a professional accreditation in 1970. Ray Lutke joined the music faculty and was appointed Head of Instrumental Music and began the first band program, The Biola Symphonic Winds, a position he held for 20 years.

1970–1982

 WRESTLING

In 1982 the wrestling team, coached by Matt Orr, had the largest squad since 1978, with 16 wrestlers on the squad. The same year, Biola had one of the most prestigious Invitational in the nation with five NCAA Division I top 20 teams. The team won two NAIA District III titles (District III wrestling, ended in 1977). In addition, in 1982, Biola held the 8th annual National Christian College Athletic Association Championships (NCCAA), the first held in the west coast.

▶ **CAMPUS SAFETY**

Biola's department of Campus Safety has been safe guarding the community of students for many years. The department's motto today continues to be to protect and to serve the Biola community.

▲ **DRAMA TEAM**

In 1977, Drama Interpretation, Reader's Theatre, Debate, and Oral Interpretation were all included under the forensics program. The drama team was sent out locally to minister to church congregations, youth groups and to aid in evangelism. The forensic team would compete with other colleges. Competition was open to anyone interested, novice to pro. In the mid-'70s, Biola was counted amongst the top ten small colleges in the nation, with a number one rating in California. Under the leadership of Todd Lewis, the team went on to win over 3,500 awards in the next 20 years.

WOMEN'S VOLLEYBALL

The women's volleyball team started in the late '60s. They participated in the Southern California Women's Intercollegiate Athletic Conference (SCWIAC) Championships in 1975 and took first place. Today, the team is ranked in the NAIA's top five.

WOMEN'S BASKETBALL

In 1981 and 1983 the women's basketball team went on to the NAIA National Tournament. The women's team has consistently displayed athletic excellence.

TRACK AND FIELD

The 1979 track season produced a turnout that Coach Colin McDougall had not experienced in many years. There were a large number of students on the team. The caliber of returnees and promising newcomers made for an exciting season. The track and field team continues to excel in the sport with athletes placing in the top ten in the 2007 NAIA Track and Field Championships.

1970—1982

NCCAA
NATIONAL
BASKETBALL CHAMPION
DIVISION I
1984

EAGLES SOARED

The Biola Eagles soared to district and national competition in almost every varsity sport. The 1982 season will be best remembered for the phenomenal success of the varsity men's basketball team coached by Howard Lyon and David Holmquist. Biola led the nation as the only undefeated team in league play, winning 39 consecutive games, named the NAIA District III champions. Rated the best all-around NAIA team in the nation, Biola drew the attention of athletes, coaches, spectators and sports reporters around the country and was publicized in such publications as *Newsweek*.

CHAPTER SIX

Seasons of Change

Just days before Clyde Cook's inauguration on October 8, 1982, a *New York Times*

headline read, "Colleges Are Warned Of Enrollment Decline".

BELL TOWER
The Bell Tower was constructed in 1986, at the center of campus using five of the original 11 bells from the downtown campus. It chimes at 9:25 a.m. daily to remind students of regular chapel attendance. The campus community also hears the chimes at noon and 5 p.m. daily. At the dedication, Sam Sutherland commented that Biolans were passing the torch to a new generation.

STATISTICS SHOWED that the number of college-aged adults would decline by as much as 25 percent over the next 15 years. And Biola was already experiencing a drop in enrollment as Generation X made its way through college.

Only one year into Biola's transition from a college to a university, Cook would be called upon to lead the school into an uncertain future. And like so many times before, storms would test the strength of the University's roots.

But Cook was no stranger to trials. The son of a sea captain and a former missionary, Cook spent his first seven years in Hong Kong. When the Japanese invaded in 1941, Cook, his parents and his five siblings were separated into three different concentration camps where they nearly starved to death.

including five of the original 11 Meneely bells used by the Bible Institute. The University used the bells to construct its iconic Bell Tower, connecting Biola's past with its present. The bells continue to chime daily at 9:25 a.m., at noon and at 5 p.m. to serve as a reminder of the University's rich heritage.

But all the momentum and excitement of Cook's first years in office couldn't shelter Biola from the coming enrollment crisis. From 1980–1989, enrollment had dropped 20 percent, from 3,181 students to 2,566. Department budgets were slashed and salaries were frozen. Schools across the nation were tightening their belts.

It was at this time that the 20-acre McNally Middle School property Biola had leased for nearly a decade came up for sale. But with enrollment down and budgets tight, it looked

DURING THESE TRANSITIONS, BIOLA CONTINUED IN ITS HISTORIC ROLE AS A LEADING VOICE FOR EVANGELICALISM.

In 1953 Cook enrolled at Biola, after turning down many basketball scholarship to other universities. After graduating, Cook and his wife, Anna Belle, who has played such an important role in their various ministries, served in the Philippines for several years and then returned to Biola, heading the missions department from 1967–1979. It was Biola's mission that would eventually lure Cook to the University from OC International, a missions agency, where he served as president from 1979–1982. When Cook took over as Biola's president, he broadened the University's understanding of missions, urging all students to see themselves as missionaries, whether in business, education or cross-cultural ministry. With his missionary mindset, Cook quickly went to work, setting several University milestones during his first year in office.

One of his early achievements included the founding of the School of Intercultural Studies, which became Biola's fourth school in 1983. That same year, the University dedicated its $2 million Welch Computer Center. Also in 1983, Talbot Theological Seminary became Talbot School of Theology, merging Biola's undergraduate and graduate programs in Bible and theology.

Cook's first year also marked Biola's 75th anniversary. For the occasion, the University returned to its former Los Angeles campus to celebrate at the Church of the Open Door, which would soon leave the downtown facility for a suburban setting. When the building was razed five years later, Biola managed to salvage key artifacts from the historic landmark,

certain that the University would lose the property. Biola needed $500,000 to secure the $4 million property by May 31, 1988.

Thirty days before the deadline, Biola only had $34,000 toward the down payment. But before the deadline approached a Biola Trustee sold his vacation home and gave the proceeds for the purchase of the McNally school. The gift soon became known as the "McNally Miracle". The additional land provided critical facilities and room for expansion in the years ahead. Other miracles followed before Biola would make its final payment on the property in 1991—a year after Kent Twitchell finished painting his famous, 30-foot tall "Jesus Mural" on Bardwell Hall.

Concerned about the declining enrollment, in 1990, Cook formed an institutional marketing council to assess Biola's strengths and weaknesses and to recommend marketing and academic program changes. In 1992, it was decided that "The Biola Hour" radio ministry would be discontinued due to lack of finances. This was a very difficult decision since "The Biola Hour" had an impact throughout the United States. In 1993, a fifth school, the School of Business, opened to better serve Biola's growing business major. In 1994, the University added its sixth school, the School of Continuing Studies, to reach undergraduate adult learners and international students.

1982–1997

Even as enrollment decline continued, Biola's leaders saw the need to make important additions to campus facilities. At the south end of campus stood eight old bungalows, built in the early 1960s as temporary housing. These humble structures had been built for $1 per square-foot, and had long since reached the end of their serviceable life. In 1990, they were replaced by Thompson Hall, a 120-bed residence hall for undergraduates, and were supplemented by Biola's first apartment buildings—Welch Hall and Li Hall. The 15 one-bedroom apartments in Welch Hall were built to meet the need for married student housing, and Li Hall added 15 two-bedroom units, each designed to house four graduate students. At the same time, a new bookstore was added, more than tripling the size of the old store, a central receiving and warehouse facility was added, and an innovative central heating, cooling, and cogeneration power plant was constructed, with more than four miles of water piping connecting all campus buildings. The facility, purchased through a bond issue, has saved Biola close to a million dollars annually.

During these transitions, Biola continued in its historic role as a leading voice for evangelicalism. In the spring of 1995, the University hosted *Jesus Under Fire* Conferences across the country in response to the Jesus Seminar's attacks on the Gospel accounts of Christ's life and teaching. In 1996, Biola hosted the *Mere Creation* conference, the first major gathering of intelligent-design proponents. That same year, the University founded the Torrey Honors Institute, an Oxford-style honors program.

By 1997, Biola had reached the highest enrollment in its 89-year history with 3,383 students. Under Cook's leadership, the University forged ahead with a $20 million capital campaign to provide essential funding for a new library.

Stronger than ever, the University had become a nationally known leader in Christian higher education, remaining deeply rooted in it mission of providing biblically centered education, scholarship and service. 🌿

▲ WELCH COMPUTER CENTER
Robert Welch and his wife, Bitsy funded the $2 million state-of-the-art Welch Computer Center. It opened in 1984 providing students with computer resources as technology was revolutionizing the nation. In the same year, a computer science major was added. Eventually, Biola became a showcase school for Macintosh computers in the '80s. Robert Welch died in August 1992 after serving on the Board of Trustees for more than 30 years.

◀ SCHOOL OF INTERCULTURAL STUDIES
President Cook founded the School of Intercultural Studies (SICS) in 1983 of which Dr. Marvin Mayers of Wycliffe Bible Translators became dean. Programs offered by SICS are the Master's degree in Intercultural Studies and Missions, the Doctor of Missiology degree, a field course program and the Doctor of Education program.

1982–2007

CLYDE COOK

Born in 1935, son of a sea captain and former missionary, Clyde Cook grew up in Hong Kong. When the Japanese invaded in 1941, he, his parents and five siblings were imprisoned for six months in three separate concentration camps. In 1942, he was reunited with his poverty stricken family in South Africa.

They later settled in Laguna Beach, Calif., where Cook excelled on his high school basketball team. As the 1953 California Interscholastic Federation's "Basketball Player of the Year", Cook received lucrative scholarship offers from 13 colleges and universities. He planned to play for the University of Southern California, but, two weeks before classes started, he began to rethink his priorities.

He enrolled at Biola College to prepare for a professional Christian ministry. There, he met his wife, Anna Belle Lund ('55), and earned three degrees: a bachelor's degree in Bible, a master of divinity and a master of theology. After a five-year stint as Biola's athletic director and coach of the men's sports teams, he, Anna Belle and their two young children, Laura and Craig, left as missionaries

to the Philippines. But they returned four years later for Cook to head Biola's missions department, which he did for 12 years. In 1979, Cook was appointed the president of Overseas Crusades, a missions agency (now called OC International).

Biola's Board of Trustees watched as Cook grew Overseas Crusades and increased its financial stability. So, when then-president Dick Chase resigned in 1982, the Board invited Cook to be Biola's seventh president.

Dr. Clyde Cook assumed the presidency of Biola University in 1982 when the school was in transition from a college to university.

Cook addressed the school's new mindset and focused on the structure and strategy for the new Christian university as it entered a decade of declining enrollment and dwindling finances.

Cook served for seven years on the Board of Directors of the Christian College Coalition and one year as its chair. He also served for six years on the Board of Directors of the American Association of Independent Colleges and Universities, and served as the president of that organization for two years. He served on the Western Association of Schools and Colleges accreditation task force. He also served several years as a member of the steering committee for the Fellowship of Evangelical Seminary Presidents and for six years on the executive committee of the Association of Independent Colleges and Universities of California.

In 2006 Cook announced retirement after twenty-five years of service. He noted that he wanted to allow a new president to usher in Biola's 100-year anniversary.

▲ TESOL

In 1991, the Biola in China program and the TESOL (Teachers of English of Other Languages) and Applied Linguistics Departments were added. David and Elaine Crane (pictured) began serving in China as missionaries in 1990.

◀ MCNALLY CAMPUS

Acquisition of McNally campus took place on May 31, 1988. Ken Casey, Vice President of Financial Affair, and Dr. Robert F. Crawford, Vice President and Chief Information Officer spearheaded the project. Biola had leased the property since 1978. Dr. Crawford let the negotiations with the school board to buy the property. Biola needed $500,000 to secure the $4 million property by May 31, 1988. Thirty days before the deadline, President Cook only had $34,000 toward the down payment. But before the deadline a trustee sold his vacation home and gave the proceeds for the purchase of the McNally school. The gift soon became known as the "McNally Miracle". Many other friends of Biola made the first payment possible, including Mr. and Mrs. Robert Welch and Mrs. Irene Li. The property accommodates faculty offices, some university services and academics departments meeting the needs of a growing student body. The final payment was made on the property in 1991.

In 1996, with 145 programs in 11 different degrees offered at Biola, students from all backgrounds are drawn to the school. Since the late '90s, the University has experienced 49 percent growth and enrollment in 2007 measured 6,000 students.

▲ CHRISTMAS TREE LIGHTING

The alumni department started the Christmas Tree Lighting tradition in 1985 as an event that would launch the Christmas season on campus and encourage alumni to return with their families and students to celebrate. Originally the large California redwood next to the science building was selected but it was too delicate. So they started decorating a tree that was planted just for the purpose of the tree lighting directly across from the corner of the science building (bell tower area) but that tree was removed in the 1990s. From then on, the tree next to Crowell Hall was used. This annual event attracts hundreds of alumni.

◄ TRIUMPH

Jeff Kennedy joined the music faculty in 1983, to direct the Biola University Singers. In 1988, "Triumph" is organized and directed by Jeff Kennedy for eight years. The group was among Biola's most recognized music groups.

1982–1997

↑▶ THOMPSON HALL, LI AND WELCH APARTMENTS

Three housing buildings were constructed in 1990—Thompson Hall, Li and Welch Apartments. Thompson was in memory of Trustee, Bob Thompson's parents. Welch and Li were dedicated to supporters of Biola—Irene Li (pictured in black), Fook Kong and Robert Welch. Thompson Hall, is a three-story building housing 150 students both male and female, in suite-style living. The two-story apartment building, Li Apartments, is approximately 1,050-square-feet. Welch Apartments provides 15 on-campus one-bedroom apartments. In the last decade, Biola has purchased apartment buildings close to campus - Lido Mirada, Beachcomber, Tradewind and Tropicana Apartments.

↑ TALBOT SCHOOL OF THEOLOGY

Talbot Theological Seminary becomes Talbot School of Theology in 1983.

▲ COLLEGE LIFE

As student enrollment started to increase in 1996, college life was alive and vibrant. As students experienced their newfound independence they also experienced financial responsibilities, so they called on their parents for social money.

◄ "THE WORD" MURAL

Biola's 30-foot tall mural of Christ was donated and painted by internationally acclaimed muralist, Kent Twitchell in 1990. The mural was designed by Twitchell and painted with the assistance of art students. The two shadows symbolize the Trinity. Jesus' hands are the same color as the pages of the Bible symbolizing the Word became flesh.

◄ SCHOOL SPIRIT

Students, with red and white painted faces, enjoy a Biola basketball game. The games attract many students during the basketball season. Biolans take pride in cheering for "The Eagles". For a long time Biola had cheerleaders to assist in stirring up school spirit, but the program was discontinued in the late '80s. In 2007, Biola introduced a new cheerleading team.

1982 — 1997

▲ "THE BIOLA HOUR" DISCONTINUED

"The Biola Hour" radio ministry, produced in its later years by Al Sanders since 1952, was discontinued in the summer of 1992. "In its life-span," Cook wrote upon its ending, "'The Biola Hour' saved, counseled, nurtured, and encouraged thousands of men, women and children across North America."

▼ BIOLA CONNECTIONS

Biola's alumni magazine was started in 1986. With a current circulation of over 50,000, *Biola Connections* reaches alumni around the world. In 2007, it changed its name to *Biola Magazine*.

▲ SCHOOL OF BUSINESS

The Crowell School of Business was added in 1993, and housed in the Metzger Administration building, in order to accommodate growing student demand for the business major and to produce graduates who are ethically sound and technically competent. Professor Henry Warren, former chair of Biola's business department, and Larry Strand, dean of the school, were responsible for making the School of Business a reality. Bill Billard, Chairman of the Board of Trustees, was also instrumental in this endeavor by providing funding. The William G. Billard Conference Room in the School of Business was dedicated in October of 1997. The School of Business developed into a school by steady growth from emphasis to major to department to school.

▲ ELLIS PARK

In March of 1993 construction began on Ellis Park, to provide an outdoor recreation area for students. It included a picnic area, barbecue grills and a basketball and volleyball court. Franklin Ellis donated the $200,000 needed. Hope Hall currently occupies the park's location.

▶ BOOKSTORE

The dedication of Biola's new 7,200-square-foot bookstore, in May of 1991, demonstrated Biola's continuing commitment to quality university resources. The new bookstore was more than three times the size of its predecessor and served the community as well. Auxiliary Services and Student Affairs also moved into the new building and the school added a new warehouse and a central plant.

▲ *JESUS UNDER FIRE*

In the spring of 1995, the Alumni Association hosted the successful Jesus Under Fire Conference attended by over 1,500 people; additional Jesus Under Fire conferences followed that year. The speakers, Talbot professors Drs. Mike Wilkins and J.P. Moreland, used the arguments presented in their book, *Jesus Under Fire*, to defend the Gospel accounts of Jesus' life. The book was named one of the top ten books of 1995 by *Christianity Today*.

◄ SIXTH SCHOOL ADDED

In 1994, Biola added its sixth school—the School of Continuing Studies, which later becomes the School of Professional Studies. Programs offered under this school are the Biola Organizational Leadership Degree (BOLD), started in 1991; the department of International Student Education (ISE); and, in association with Talbot, the Master of Arts in Christian Apologetics, newly created in 1997.

University chapels and conferences are intended to bring the Biola community together regularly for worship, spiritual nurture and education regarding relevant issues facing us in our lives. The overall program brings a unique distinction to the ethos of Biola as a Christian university. Chapel attendance is required of all students. Chapels are organized by the Chaplain's Office and the AS Chapel Board. Many renowned speakers have spoken at chapels from Chuck Swindoll to Luis Palau and Toni Eareckson Tada. Chapels are held on Monday, Wednesday and Friday in the gymnasium from 9:30 a.m.–10:30 a.m.

▾ TORREY HONORS INSTITUTE

Torrey Honors Institute, whose purpose is the formation of biblically-centered intellectual leadership, enrolled its first class of freshmen in the fall of 1996. Dr. John Mark Reynolds developed the honors level program. The program is dedicated to forming leaders through the study of the master works of Western civilization, with a special emphasis on the Bible and Christian authors. The program has grown and today the average applicant is among the top ten percent of students planning to attend Biola.

▲ GROWTH

Enrollment continued to grow in 1996 with 145 programs in 11 different degrees offered at Biola. M.A. in Education was reinstated. Students from all backgrounds are drawn to Biola for its wide range of programs.

▲ HIGHEST ENROLLMENT

In 1997, Biola reached its highest fall enrollment of students, 3,383, in its history. Certain facilities, like the library, no longer provided sufficient accommodations for students' needs. Plans for expansion were underway.

1982—1997

▶ ATHLETICS

There were seven men's and eight women's teams providing a great sense of community and camaraderie among students, faculty, administrators, trustees, alumni and the general public. Since 1983, 44 All-Americans and 29 Academic All-Americans have been honored at Biola. The Men's Basketball Team has won the NAIA District III Championship five times in that span of time. Alumni such as Todd Worrell ('82), recipient of The 1995 Coaches Award from the University for excellence in baseball, reflect the caliber of athletes the department produces. Both Todd and Tim ('89) Worrell went on to pitch for the major leagues.

▶ STUDENT MISSIONARY UNION

The Student Missionary Union (SMU) marked its 70th anniversary in 1993. A hallmark of Biola, SMU manages the largest annual student-run mission conference on the west coast. In the late 1960s, President Cook, advisor of SMU at the time, 1967 SMU President Bob Thune and Keith Phillips of World Opportunities were instrumental in developing a greater interest in missions among students. Over 250 Biola students traveled each week to South Central Los Angeles to minister to inner-city children. Jacinda Abrams, student director of the 1997 conference, worked with 30 students to coordinate 100 missions organizations, speakers and the Biola community to help students understand how to further God's kingdom in the world. SMU continues to send over 30 mission teams annually around the world.

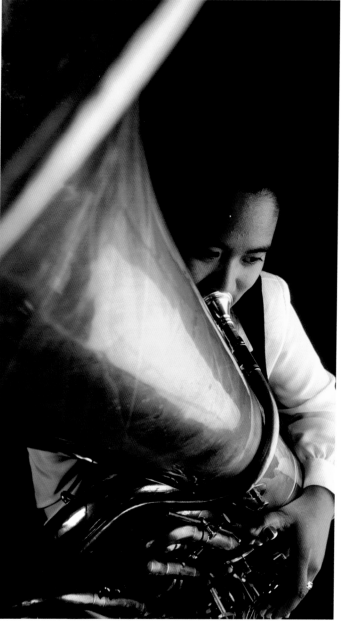

▲ CERAMIC/SCULPTURE STUDIO OPENS

In order to make room for the new library, built on the site of the Metzger parking lot, a new Ceramic/Sculpture Studio was built in 1997 to replace the old Art Barn. The new structure housed ceramics and metal sculpture among other art activities, and was dedicated in October 1997. The art department, chaired by Barry Krammes, also celebrated its 25th year as a major. Earlier in May, the department was accredited by the National Association of Schools of Art & Design.

▶ MUSIC EXCELLENCE

Biola equips students for fine performances in the area of music. Many of the faculty in the music department, now called the Conservatory of Music, are professionals in their field, raising the caliber of the programs offered. Accomplished and renown alumni Earle Patriarco ('89), rising opera performer, and Ruth (Morris) Gray ('83), church music minister, have benefited from their professors' real-world experiences.

ACCREDITATION

Western Association of Schools and Colleges continues to reconfirm Biola University's accreditation. In 1995 and in 2006 Biola received the maximum accreditation, citing the university operates with admirable openness and integrity. Biola's Rosemead and Talbot were also reaccredited for the maximum years.

CHAPTER SEVEN

Deeply Rooted for the Next Century

El Niño wasn't the only storm to hit America in 1998. Millennials—the largest generation in U.S. history—were arriving on campuses across the country, creating a flood of tech-savvy students who would make new products, like Google and Apple, household names.

FLUOR FOUNTAIN OF FAITH

Construction begins on a new fountain in 1999. The project was funded by a gracious gift by Marjorie Fluor Moore, a Biola friend. The fountain would be called the Fluor Fountain of Faith and created a new place for students to congregate and relax or study in the sun.

HAVING WEATHERED the declining enrollments of the early '80s and mid-'90s, Biola was entering a period of unprecedented growth. By the end of 2007, the University would nearly double its enrollment. But the late '90s marked a period of reflection for Biola.

In 1998, while celebrating its 90th anniversary, the University sponsored a series of lectures to answer the question, "What does it mean to be a Christian university in the 21st century?" Noted evangelical scholars such as theologian J.I. Packer, philosopher Dallas Willard and historian George Marsden came to campus to interact with Biola's faculty on the question.

In 1999, spiritual formation courses were added to the freshmen curriculum. And professors pursued ways to integrate the Bible with their field of study to provide additional integration beyond the 30 units of Bible required for graduation.

This renewed commitment to biblically centered education was attractive to students and parents, causing enrollment to soar. The Torrey Honors Institute at Biola, which was already attracting the nation's top academic Christian freshmen, reached its 240-student limit in 1999. And the master's program in philosophy and religion, whose students had a 98 percent acceptance rate when applying to graduate school, had nearly 100 students in its program and had graduated more than 170 students in less than ten years.

FOR 100 YEARS, BIOLA UNIVERSITY HAS REMAINED TRUE TO ITS MISSION OF PROVIDING BIBLICALLY CENTERED EDUCATION, SCHOLARSHIP AND SERVICE—EQUIPPING MEN AND WOMEN IN MIND AND CHARACTER TO IMPACT THE WORLD FOR THE LORD JESUS CHRIST.

Among the issues discussed at the conference was the threat of postmodernism—a reaction to the assumed certainty of objective truth commonly featured in modernism. Though difficult to define, postmodernism challenged the notion of absolute truth. For Biola, this movement threatened to undermine biblical Christianity.

So as the University stepped forward into the next century, Biola's leadership committed to a three-fold purpose: to prepare graduates to be strong in mind and character, equipped to serve in their professions, the church and the world; to produce scholarship that confronts current philosophies and cultural secularism; and to stand as a beacon of faith, demonstrating a commitment to think and act as Christians.

The University began sponsoring apologetics events, such as the Defending the Faith Lecture Series, where faculty members from Talbot School of Theology's philosophy of religion and ethics master's program led lectures for students and lay Christians.

Biola also made a commitment to impact the television and film industries. A 120-member studio task force of media professionals was assembled to help make inroads into the entertainment industry. And Biola dedicated the first phase of its new television and film studio on September 11, 1998, with the 4,200-square-foot Warren Studio named after TV producer Michael Warren, chairman of the studio task force.

The arts and sciences also flourished. With more than 100 students, the music department continued to emphasize music education rooted in the classical tradition taught by stellar faculty, including its famous Artist-In-Residence, Menahem Pressler, founder and pianist of the Beaux Arts Trio. And in the sciences, 90 percent of biology graduates who applied to graduate school were accepted, as were 75 percent of those who applying to medical school, attracting even more students to the program.

By the year 2000, nearly 2,500 undergraduate students enrolled at Biola. The student growth rate was nearly 6 percent annually, and Biola's facilities were feeling the squeeze. To manage the growth, President Cook, along with the University Planning Group, plotted the school's course of growth, which would include several new building projects and launch a new vision to be a global center for Christian thought and spiritual renewal. Over the next six years, Biola would add nearly a half million square feet of floor space to the campus.

In 2001, the University opened its new 98,000-square-foot library, which, with its lighted beacon, became the centerpiece of the campus. Rosemead School of Psychology took over the remodeled Rose Library in 2002. In 2003, the 101,000-square-foot residence hall, Hope Hall, was ready to accommodate 426 students. And in 2004, Chase Gymnasium received an 8,894-square-foot expansion, along with a raised synthetic turf soccer field and track atop a new parking structure, and a new fitness center. Horton Hall was rebuilt in 2005 into a four-story, 89,000-square-foot residence hall housing 416 students. And in 2006, the

32,000-square-foot Crowell Business Building was built to house the Crowell School of Business.

By 2006, Biola had never experienced better times. Ranked by *U.S. News & World Report* as a "National University"—the only evangelical school the magazine grouped with the "major leagues of higher education"—Biola was one of the fast-growing universities in the nation with student enrollment over 5,500 in 2006. It boasted new campus buildings, attracted top Christian scholars among its faculty, and one of the largest operating budgets in the Council for Christian Colleges & Universities.

With all of this momentum, President Cook decided the time was right to announce his retirement. After 25 years as president, Cook wanted to hand over what he called his "sacred trust" to a new leader who could take Biola into its second century.

On May 10, 2007, after a national seven-month search, Dr. Barry H. Corey was selected as Biola's eighth president. He joins a long line of trailblazers in Christian education—from Lyman Stewart and R.A. Torrey to Sam Sutherland and Clyde Cook.

For 100 years, Biola University has remained true to its mission of providing biblically centered education, scholarship and service—equipping men and women in mind and character to impact the world for the Lord Jesus Christ. From 35 students in 1908 to more than 5,800 in 2008, Biola will enter its second century deeply rooted in a tradition that honors Christ as the source of all wisdom and knowledge and challenges its community of students, alumni, faculty and staff to follow in His steps. ❧

▶ SINGSPIRATION
Started in the late '80s, this Sunday evening gathering serves as a time for the Biola community to devote an hour to worship.

THEN GOD SAID, "LET THERE BE LIGHT"; AND THE

1:3-4

▶ LIBRARY THEME

In 2000, the groundbreaking for the new library took place. The library's theme incorporates light through scripture verses, expansive windows and the signature beacon, which floods the library with natural sunlight. The scripture inscribed on the inner part of the beacon on the third floor is Genesis 1:3–4. The library was completed in 2001.

▼ NEW LIBRARY

The 98,000-square-foot, tri-level library, has a growing collection of 300,000 volumes and grants students access to 19,000 full text periodicals. The library also has 23 study rooms available for students to study and a two-story periodical reading room with mezzanine, providing additional studying environments. The upper-level study terrace and the middle-level Heritage Court offer more than 100 outdoor study spaces with wireless network connectivity.

ARE ASKING, "WHO CAN SHOW
NY GOOD?" LET THE LIGHT OF
FACE SHINE UPON US O LORD.
PSALM 4:6

THE LORD IS MY LIGHT AND MY
SALVATION-WHOM SHALL I FEAR?
PSALM 27:1

ARISE, SHINE; FOR YO
COME, AND THE GLOF
HAS RISEN UP
ISAIAH

▶ SWIMMING

Biola offers a competitive swim program. In 2007, the men and women teams both placed seventh at NAIA Swim Championships.

▶ SOFTBALL

In 2002, the women's softball team placed second at NAIA Nationals. In 2007, Biola reached the NAIA Region II tournament for the third straight year and sixth time in the last eight seasons, and finished fourth in the Golden State Athletic Conference.

▼ TENNIS

In addition to a team, the women's tennis program includes a variety of community programs offered year round, including singles and doubles tournament, community leagues and wheelchair tennis. The men's tennis program was reinstated at Biola in 2006. In 2007, the women's tennis team was one of 12 NAIA squads to be named an All-Academic Team by the Intercollegiate Tennis Association for the fifth straight year. The addition of six tennis courts allows Biola to host matches.

▶ COACH HOLMQUIST

In 2000, Biola's basketball coach and Athletic Director, Dave Holmquist became the youngest college basketball coach, at any level, to win 500 games in the U.S.—one week after his 47th birthday. News coverage descended upon Biola as Los Angeles papers covered the feat as well as prime time news stations like ABC channel 7 and KCAL 9.

BASEBALL TEAM WINS

In 2001, the baseball team won their fourth GSAC (Golden State Athletic Conference) Championship in four years ('98, '99, '00, '01). That same year, softball won first in the league, as did men's soccer. The baseball team won the GSAC Championship again in 2001 and 2005. Today, Biola's baseball team has 29 members and is currently led by Coach John Verhoeven. Up to date, 28 baseball players and 34 basketball players have moved on to play professional ball.

◀ BIOLA PROFESSIONAL BUILDING

The Professional Building purchased in La Mirada houses the Biola Counseling Center and the School of Professional Studies. The Biola Counseling Center provides counseling services for students, faculty, and staff as well as the community.

▲ ART GALLERY

The University Art Gallery, first housed in Metzger, hosts traveling national art shows, but it is best known for its regular senior openings and shows. The gallery moved to its current location in the mid-'80s. Monthly the gallery has exhibits on display. The gallery allows current students an opportunity to publicize and reveal their "final" artistic vision. The gallery is operated by the Department of Art.

◀ MUSIC IN WORSHIP PROGRAM

The ribbon cutting for a new Music in Worship facility took place October 26, 2004. The newly refurbished facility, which once housed University Facility Services, includes two ensemble rehearsal/recording spaces and seven teaching and practice studios. Yamaha Corporation, made it possible to equip the facility with state-of-the-art keyboards, recording and sound reinforcement equipment, amplifiers and instruments. Shure Incorporated generously donated microphones. The building provides students with a place to rehearse in both acoustic and amplified environments. Lessons in guitar, bass, and keyboard are also offered in the new facility. Enrollment for the program has met the department's expectations.

HOPE HALL
The ribbon cutting ceremony in 2003 drew many to visit Hope Hall, the 101,000-square-foot dorm, and the largest dormitory to date. It has a lobby dedicated to Biola's original campus on Hope and 6th. The four-story building houses 426 students equipped with two elevators and three stairwells. Students also get to enjoy the outdoor amphitheater with formal seating for nearly 200, and informal seating close to 400.

◄ NEW FIELD
The $5.5 million state-of-the-art synthetic turf field was built in 2004, with a parking structure underneath giving students over 550 new spaces to park and the entire community a beautiful track and field where to practice, play and train.

▼ CHASE GYMNASIUM EXPANSION
In 2004, Biola made plans to expand Chase Gymnasium updating its amenities, adding staff offices, and 800 stadium-style seats. The expansion added 8,894-square feet and increased seating capacity from 2,400 to 3,200 with a balcony providing students with more room to worship.

REMODELED CAFETERIA

Biola's cafeteria was remodeled in 2005. Changed from the average cafeteria, the new café is a dining experience. It consists of six different stations where students can enjoy grilled food, pizza, specialty salads, or home-style foods in addition to an assortment of breads, cereals and a salad bar. All the stations are all you can eat and represent the best of Bon Appétit. Bon Appétit Management Company is an on-site custom restaurant company that provides café and catering services to corporations, colleges and universities, and specialty venues. Bon Appétit's goal is to be known for its culinary expertise and commitment to socially responsible practices.

THE EDDY

Sponsored by Social Board, the Eddy is a free concert series that takes place on Thursday nights outside Common Grounds. Local bands and musicians from Biola use the Eddy as an opportunity for exposure, experience, and expression.

MOCK ROCK

Students form groups to perform musical skits in front of fluorescent lights for Mock Rock—an annual, dramatic lip-syncing competition.

◀ HORTON HALL

Horton Hall was built in 2006 over the tiny building that once housed just 123 women and now stands five stories tall, towering over the campus. It now houses 400 men and women.

▲ CONSERVATORY OF MUSIC

In 2003, the music department took on a new name, The Biola University Conservatory of Music. George Boespflug became the Director of the Conservatory.

◀ CROWELL SCHOOL OF BUSINESS

The Crowell School of Business was completed in 2007. The 32,000-square-foot building was the first classroom building constructed on the university's La Mirada campus since 1974. It has 12 classrooms, a computer lab, staff and faculty offices, and an outdoor eating area. The new facility was made possible by a generous gift from the Crowell Family, descendents of Lyman Stewart. (Family pictured on the right-hand side of the platform at the ribbon cutting ceremony.)

◀ COLLEGIUM

The Collegium, Latin for "Gathering Place", was built in 2004. Housed in the upper Student Union Building it gives commuter students a place to call their own. The 13,000-square-foot Collegium features home like furnishings, a fully equipped kitchen, dining area, a study area with computers, two living rooms and a fireplace.

◀ MIDNIGHT MADNESS

Midnight Madness, a tradition introduced in the late '90s, where students welcome the basketball season with this adrenaline-filled rally featuring skits, dance performances, three-point and dunk competitions, and lots of red.

◀ MAMMOTH FOSSILS FOUND

Biola received national news coverage in August 2002 when prehistoric fossils believed to be from a mammoth or mastadon were found at the new Hope Hall construction site. Anthropology students excavated a mammoth skull, tusk and full set of teeth. Since the discovery of the mammoth fossils the anthropology program has grown from four students to 41, in 2005.

1997 — 2008

GRADUATION

For the past ten years, Biola has graduated a record number of students. Spring 2007 was no exception—Biola graduated 900 students. Dr. Charles Swindoll, internationally known as a best-selling author and speaker on the "Insight for Living" radio program and chancellor of Dallas Theological Seminary, served as the commencement speaker. He is part of the list of renowned speakers Biola has attracted to commencement ceremonies, including Luis Palau, Lloyd Ogilvie, Josh McDowell ('71), James Dobson and Charles Colson. More than 50,000 graduates are impacting the world for Jesus Christ in the workforce and on the mission field. In addition, each year Biola sends out over ten summer mission teams across the world to further the Great Commission.

1997—2008

BARRY H. COREY

THE NEW CENTURY BEGINS WITH A NEW PRESIDENT

JULY 2007

Over the last century, seven presidents have prayerfully and faithfully led Biola to a place of international prominence without compromising its biblical foundation. Following the twenty-five years of leadership by Clyde Cook, I am incredibly honored and humbled to serve as Biola's eighth president and carry on the legacy of the founders and presidents before me. I am committed to lead the University community worldwide into a new century of visioning and imagining what God could do in this and coming generations.

Biola has ignited my sense of excitement and enthusiasm for joining this community as I hear the stories of those who have been shaped as servants by the mission of Biola to be a global center for Christian thought and spiritual renewal. More than ever before, we need to engage globally, we need to think Christianly and we need to be shaped in the likeness of Christ.

I have committed my new role to the Lord, covenanting with him to protect fearlessly that which is most precious in his sight, standing with my predecessors on the centrality of his inerrant Word, the exclusive saving grace of Christ, the mandate for mission and evangelism, the quality of a Biola education, and our zeal to become more like Jesus in conduct and character. These I will defend whatever the future may hold. And the future is exceedingly bright for Biola University.

Biola has not abandoned nor eroded its strong biblical roots over this 100-year history and that is an indication that its future is certain as a leading light in the world of Christian higher education. We stand at a wonderful watershed moment in Biola's history.

Biola is strategically positioned, not only in Southern California, but also around the world to make a deep and lasting impact for the Kingdom of God. I believe God will use the University in ways far beyond what we as men and women can imagine and plan. Picture Lyman Stewart's and T.C. Horton's expressions if they could see the Bible Institute of Los Angeles today. God had a greater plan in mind for the institute—Biola University.

As we embark on bold and collaborative ventures to place Biola at the vanguard of global thinking and service, we will not lose sight of the University's founding mission and vision but will work with intensity and selflessness toward that end. Our attitudes at every level of service must remain optimistic and courteous, becoming contagious to those we serve, and striving to lead less with a scepter and more with a hoe.

I believe a mark of an exemplary Christian university is to extend outward and not inward, to exist not for its own sake but for the sake of fulfilling the Great Commission. A Christian university of the 21st century must be grounded in the inerrant Truth, living in the understanding that God has called a generation of students to shape the world for Christ in ways that are creative and courageous. The community of Biola here in Southern California and around the world through students and alumni will strive to be a model of this mindset.

At Biola, we believe a Christian university is the training ground where students develop intellectually and spiritually. We pursue academic excellence so that Biola students have the preparation needed to thrive in their vocational pursuits, while equipping them spiritually to be the next generation of leaders in the church and throughout the world.

We will forge into Biola's new century by building strength upon strength, beating the drum for biblical fidelity and literacy. We need men and women who not only know God's word, but who live lives faithful to that Word, strengthened and renewed by the Holy Spirit. Building upon that which Biola cherishes and holds as its core, we will take its Kingdom calling to the next level in Christ-honoring ways, with dignity and boldness. Biola must be increasingly global minded so we do not become culturally irrelevant. We must return to the city and become a greater diverse community. Spiritual formation must remain at the heart of who we are so that Biola graduates will continue to be positioned to understand the culture and to present the truth so clearly and so passionately that the world cannot help but see through them that the Truth is Jesus Christ.

Biola's new vision to become a global center for Christian thought and spiritual renewal is bold and audacious but firmly rooted in its founding mission with a century of accomplishments to guide the future. We are poised to educate and prepare a new generation of believers who will become change agents boldly proclaiming the word of Christ for Kingdom impact.

Join me in reaffirming Biola's foundational commitment for the next 100 years to live out the mission and vision through leadership, scholarship, and service, through compassion and character to impact the world for the Lord Jesus Christ.

Barry H. Corey

University President

BARRY AND PAULA COREY

PSALM 37:3-6

Trust in the Lord and do good;
Dwell in the land and cultivate faithfulness
Delight yourself in the Lord;
And He will give you the desires of your heart.
Commit your way to the Lord,
Trust also in Him, and He will do it.
He will bring forth your righteousness as the light
And your judgment as the noonday.

(New American Standard version)

1908–2008

THIRTY-FIVE STUDENTS made up the first student body. In 1911, the Bible Institute graduated its first class—four men and two women. Within seven years of opening, the Institute's enrollment had increased dramatically, with 186 students. By 1916, the curriculum had developed sufficiently to allow students to select and pursue one of four specialized majors and, by 1918, 282 students enrolled.

As the Los Angeles metropolitan area grew, so did the student body. In 1921, the Institute had its largest student enrollment in its history—525 students.

During the time the Institute faced bankruptcy and the nation faced the Great Depression, from 1926 through 1938, enrollment grew minimally. Enrollment numbers fluctuated with about 422 students.

Finally, in 1938, after the school had paid and cleared its debt, enrollment numbers began to rise. In 1939, 429 students enrolled. The school then began to experience constant growth, reaching 800 by 1946.

After Biola moved to the new La Mirada campus in 1959, enrollment numbers swelled. There was a 6 percent growth average each year for a 20-year period.

By 1979, Biola enrolled 3,111 students. A 12-year enrollment decline then followed, from 1979 to 1990, but a period of stabilization began in the early 1990s. In 1990, a strategic effort was undertaken to turn around the enrollment decline of the 1980s through a new marketing plan and academic program changes.

Biola's growth trend began in 1995. Since then, enrollment growth has surpassed 40 percent, bringing the student population to 4,000 in the year 2000.

In 2007, Biola continues to be one of the nation's fastest-growing private universities. Its commitments to the Bible, academics and cultural engagement have all contributed to nearly doubling enrollment in the past decade, from 3,205 students to 5,752. This growth has outpaced secular schools and other Christian schools, who have experienced an average of 7 percent growth and 24 percent growth, respectively. Biola received a record number of applications for fall 2007 and enrollment neared 6,000 students.

JEAN BUCHAN, 1947
Medical Missionary to India,
Recipient of the Order of Canada

JOSH MCDOWELL, 1971
Noted author and speaker,
Internationally-known
Christian apologist

CAROLYN KOONS, 1972
Founder of the Institute for
Outreach Ministries at Azusa
Pacific University, taking over
100,000 youth on global missions

WESLEY STAFFORD, 1975
President of Compassion
International

TOKUNBOH ADEYEMO, 1975, 1976
General Secretary of the
Association of Evangelicals
in Africa

JUDGE MARYANNE G. GILLIARD, 1982
Superior Court of California,
County of Sacramento

JOHN THUNE, 1983
Senator of South Dakota

EARLE PATRIARCO, 1989
Acclaimed Opera Singer
New York Metropolitan Opera

SCOTT DERRICKSON, 1990
Hollywood Screenwriter, Producer
and Director

MICHELLE BURFORD, 1994
Founding editor of *The Oprah
Magazine*, Editor for Essence and
Latina magazines, Press Delegate

*Celebrating a Century
of Faithfulness*

SCHOOL OF ARTS AND SCIENCES

TALBOT SCHOOL OF THEOLOGY

ROSEMEAD SCHOOL OF PSYCHOLOGY

SCHOOL OF INTERCULTURAL STUDIES

CROWELL SCHOOL OF BUSINESS

SCHOOL OF PROFESSIONAL STUDIES

SCHOOL OF EDUCATION

800 OK BIOLA | WWW.BIOLA.EDU | SOUTHERN CALIFORNIA

BIOLA
UNIVERSITY

TIMELINE

1908–2008

1908	Founding of the Bible Institute of Los Angeles by Lyman Stewart and T.C. Horton.
1911	First class graduated with six students.
1912	Dr. R.A. Torrey called as first Dean.
1913	Cornerstone laid for the Institute building at Sixth and Hope Streets in downtown Los Angeles.
1916	Hunan Bible Institute established as the Bible Institute of China.
1921	First three-year course offered.
1929	Dr. W.P. White assumed office as the first president.
1932	Dr. Louis T. Talbot became the second president.
1935	Paul Rood became the third president.
1936	First four-year courses offered.
1938	Dr. Talbot assumed the presidency for a second time.
1945	The School of Missionary Medicine founded by Dr. Leonie Soubirou.
1952	Dr. Samuel H. Sutherland appointed the fifth president.
	Talbot Theological Seminary inaugurated with Dr. Charles L. Feinberg as its first Dean.
1957	Groundbreaking ceremonies held for the new La Mirada campus.
1958	Sutherland Hall completed as the first building on the new campus.
1959	Official move to the new campus.

1966	The institution renamed Biola Schools and Colleges.
1970	Dr. J. Richard Chase selected as sixth president.
1972	The institution renamed Biola College.
1977	The programs of Rosemead Graduate School of Professional Psychology acquired.
1981	Biola College becomes Biola University.
1982	Dr. Clyde Cook inaugurated as seventh president.
1983	The addition of the School of Intercultural Studies and World Missions.
1985	New university structure completed with four schools now named: School of Arts and Sciences, Talbot School of Theology, Rosemead School of Psychology and School of Intercultural Studies.
1987	Carnegie Commission on Higher Education classified Biola University as a Doctorate Granting II Institution.
1993	The addition of Crowell School of Business.
1994	The addition of the School of Professional Studies.
2001	The new library is completed.
2003	Hope Hall is completed.
2006	New five-story Horton Hall replaces original two-story building.
2007	Dr. Barry H. Corey selected as eighth president.
	Crowell Business Building is completed.
	The addition of the School of Education—Biola's seventh school.

ACKNOWLEDGEMENTS

EXECUTIVE ANNIVERSARY PLANNING COMMITTEE:
Ken Bascom (Facilities Planning, '72)
Rick Bee (Alumni Relations, '79, T'90, '01)
Rich ('68) and Dianne Buhler ('67)
Dietrich Buss (Professor, History and Political Science, '63)
Peggy Campbell ('82)
Heather Cordell (Stewardship and Resource Development)
David ('54) and Elaine Crane ('53)
Marcy Guevara
    (Integrated Marketing Communications, '06)
Ron Hafer (Chaplain's Office, '61, T'75)
Stan Jantz, Member, Board of Trustees ('73)
    and Karin Jantz ('73)
Susan Kaneshiro (Human Resources)
Ed Lehman, Member, Board of Trustees ('57)
Irene Neller (Integrated Marketing Communications)
Dave Peters (Professor, History and Political Science)
Sherry Power ('67)
Jack Schwarz (Interim Vice President of Undergraduate
    Education, '61)
Brian Shook (President's Office, '92)
Steve Smith (Alumni Relations, '05)
Victoria Trevithick
    (Integrated Marketing Communications, '05)
Brenda Velasco
    (Integrated Marketing Communications, '99)
Sue Whitehead (Library, '74)

WRITERS & EDITORS: Barry H. Corey, University President;
Irene Neller, Senior Director of Integrated Marketing
Communications; Jason Newell, Copy Editor ('02); Lisa
O'Neil, Guest Contributor; Holly Pivec, University Editor
('99, T'05); Michelle Rindels, Biola student ('09); Paul Rood II,
Adjunct Faculty of Political Science; Brenda Velasco,
Centennial Manager ('99); Rob Westervelt, Director of
Brand Management and Editor of Biola Magazine (T'97)

UNIVERSITY CONSULTANTS AND CONTRIBUTORS:
Ken Bascom, Senior Director of Facilities Planning ('72);
Clyde Cook, President Emeriti ('57, T'60, '62) and Anna Belle
Cook ('55); David ('54) and Elaine Crane ('53), Alumni; Fred
Sanders, Associate Professor of Theology; Jack Schwarz,
Interim Vice Provost of Undergraduate Education ('61)

LEAD BOOK DESIGNER & PHOTOGRAPHER:
Michael Musser, Senior Graphic Designer and University
Photographer ('05)

BOOK DESIGN SUPPORT: Breanna Fowler, Manager,
Design Studio ('05); Brian Miller, Creative Director ('95);
Jessica Nelson, Graphic Designer ('05)

BOOK LAYOUT SUPPORT: Brian Miller, Creative Director
('95); Jessica Nelson, Graphic Designer ('05)

RESEARCH SUPPORT: Flo Ebling, Supervisor, Serials/
Interlibrary Loan ('71, '74); Marcy Guevara, Centennial
Assistant ('06); Michelle Rindels, Biola student ('09);
Sarah Trainor, Biola student ('08); Brenda Velasco,
Centennial Manager ('99); Sue Whitehead, Librarian,
Systems/Archivist ('74)

REVIEW SUPPORT: Ken Bascom, Senior Director, Facilities
Planning and Construction ('72); Clyde Cook, President
Emeriti ('57, T'60, '62) and Anna Belle Cook ('55); Fred
Sanders, Associate Professor of Theology, Torrey Honors
Institute; Irene Neller, Senior Director of Integrated
Marketing Communications; Jason Newell, Copy Editor
('02); Holly Pivec, University Editor ('99, T'05); Brenda
Velasco, Centennial Manager ('99); Rob Westervelt, Director
of Brand Management and Editor of Biola Magazine (T'97);
Wesley K. Willmer, Vice President, Advancement

PHOTO CREDITS: Alumni Department; Church of the
Open Door, Glendora, Calif.; University Archives

Special thanks to all Biola University alumni who are serving Jesus Christ and fulfilling the Great Commission. Matthew 28:19

Biola now